May God Bless you.

Jeff Schreve

Acts 24:15

The Promise of Eternity

From the sermon series

Forever and Ever: The Reality of Eternal Heaven and Eternal Hell

Dr. Jeff Schreve

The Promise of Eternity
From the sermon series *Forever and Ever: The Reality of Eternal Heaven and Eternal Hell*
Copyright © 2022 by Jeff Schreve

ISBN: 979-8-218-09340-2

From His Heart Ministries books may be ordered by contacting

From His Heart Ministries
P.O. Box 7267
Texarkana, TX 75505
903-838-8329
www.fromhisheart.org

Printed in the United States of America

CONTENTS

INTRODUCTION

I am excited to know that this book is in your hands. The truths contained in this reading are critically important as they deal with the subject of eternity. You see, when God made us, He made us to live forever. He sent His Son to die on the cross for our sins so that we could be forgiven, made righteous, and spend forever with Him in heaven. Everyone who receives Christ, receives the priceless gift of eternal life.

In 1979 - 1980, I was a senior in high school. I was living for self, pleasure, sports, and personal achievement. I was not horrible by the world's standards or personally unhappy, but I was spiritually lost with no hope of heaven.

On a Monday night in January, I heard a man share his testimony. He was an athlete who liked to play sports, drink beer, and chase girls. He was my kind of guy, so I listened intently to what he had to say. As he shared about giving his life to Christ, I began to ponder what exactly that meant for me.

Later that night, alone in my bedroom, the Holy Spirit of God convicted my heart of sin and showed me my future without Christ—a future in hell. The Holy Spirit revealed to me how I needed a personal relationship with Jesus. Head knowledge concerning Christ was not making any difference in my life. I needed heart knowledge. I needed to know the Lord Jesus in a genuine, personal, saving way.

So, I got down on my knees by my bed and humbly gave my life to Jesus Christ, the Son of God and God the Son. My prayer was simple but sincere, "Save me, Jesus. Save me, Jesus." And do you know what He did? He answered my prayer and saved my soul! He is the Savior, after all, and He will save anybody who will call upon His name in repentance and faith. He came into my life that night and began a good work in me that continues to this x!

My prayer for you as you read this book is that the Lord would speak to your heart about your eternity. I want you to "make your calling and election sure" (2 Peter 1:10). Heaven is real—and so is hell. There is eternal life in Christ, and there is eternal death without Him. God does not want us to have a *hope so, maybe so, guess so* salvation. He wants us to have a *know so* salvation (see I belong to Him and will be with Him in heaven when we die.

The Bible is clear. The Lord is "not wishing for any to perish but for all to come to repentance" (2 Peter 3:9). Jesus died a brutal death on the cross for us, so that we could live eternally with Him. It is truly *amazing grace* that opens the door to eternal heaven. And it is truly *amazing folly* that rejects or ignores God's only Son and Man's only Savior.

May you be enlightened, encouraged, convicted, comforted, and drawn closer to Jesus as you take His Word and His warnings to heart. May you endeavor to live your life each day to the glory of God so you can hear Him say to you the two words that truly matter, "Well done!"

Dr. Jeff Schreve
Pastor
Texarkana, Texas

CHAPTER ONE

Life and the Afterlife

"Now it came about that the poor man died and he was carried away by the angels to Abraham's bosom; and the rich man also died and was buried. And in Hades he lifted up his eyes, being in torment, and saw Abraham far away, and Lazarus in his bosom." Luke 16:22-23

Tombstones are what you see in cemeteries. Basically, tombstones tell you the person's name. They give the date they were born and the date they died. And then, sometimes they give some information about the person. They may have a little quip in there; it could be humorous, or it could be very serious. Dr. James Dobson's father's tombstone just has these two words: "He Prayed." Short but powerful.

I ran across some tombstones that were maybe a little bit less than pious and honoring and sacred, but you might have heard some of these, too.

There's a tombstone in England. It's the tombstone of Anna Wallace. It says this: "The children of Israel wanted bread, and the LORD sent them manna. Old clerk Wallace wanted a wife, and the devil sent him Anna." I don't think they had a very good marriage.

I found this one for Lester Moore. He was buried in Tombstone, Arizona. "Here lies Lester Moore, four slugs from a forty-four; no less, no more."

How about this one from London, England? "Here lies Ann Mann, who lived an old maid, but died an old

Mann." That's kind of mean, isn't it? You know her husband didn't write it!

And then, this one, on a tombstone in England: "Here beneath this pile of stones lies all that's left of Sally Jones. Her name was Smith, not Jones, but Jones was used to rhyme with stones." You're really hurting for text when you come up with that epitaph.

And then this startling one at a cemetery outside of London: "Passersby! Stop and think! I'm in eternity, and you're on the brink." All of us are on the brink. All of those who are in the cemetery, they have passed into eternity.

This book is titled *Forever and Ever: The Reality of Eternal Heaven and Eternal Hell.* Now, the mind has a hard time really grasping the concept of eternity, of forever and ever and ever and ever. But, when God made you and fashioned you, He made you and fashioned you to live forever. And there are two places to go after you leave this life. You're either going to go to eternal heaven, or you're going to go to eternal hell.

I love what my friend, evangelist Marine Tim Lee says: "Listen! You don't have to go to hell, and you don't have to go to heaven, but you can't stay here." You can't stay on earth. And all of us are going to pass from this life. We're on the brink right now. Where are we going to go?

Now, did Jesus believe in an eternal heaven and in an eternal hell? Certainly, He did. He preached about heaven, and He preached about hell. And, interestingly, if you read in the gospels, He spent more time on the subject of hell than He did on the subject of heaven. Both are real places. The reason Jesus talked more about hell is because hell is a real place, and real people go there—and He doesn't want anyone to go there. So, He warns us about hell.

Now, in Luke chapter 16, He speaks mainly to the Pharisees. He's speaking to a crowd, but He's really pinpointing to the Pharisees about life and the afterlife. The Pharisees had gotten things so wrong. So, Jesus tells them a story, a shocking story, probably not a real situation, probably a parable, but it's a shocking story that they heard, and it really was pinpointed: "This is you, Mr. Pharisee. And this is what is going to happen to you unless you repent."

Luke chapter 16, beginning in verse 19 reads, "Now there was a certain rich man ..." That's kind of the flavor of parables. There is a certain rich man. "… and he habitually dressed in purple and fine linen, gaily living in splendor every day." (He was a filthy rich guy.) "And a certain poor man named Lazarus was laid at his gate covered with sores. And longing to be fed with the crumbs which were falling from the rich man's table; besides, even the dogs were coming and licking his sores." (How gross!) "Now it came about that the poor man died, and he was carried away by the angels to Abraham's bosom; and the rich man also died and was buried. And in Hades he lifted up his eyes, being in torment, and saw Abraham far away and Lazarus in his bosom. And he cried out and said, 'Father Abraham, have mercy on me, and send Lazarus that he may dip the tip of his finger in water and cool off my tongue, for I am in agony in this flame.' But Abraham said, 'Child, remember that during your life you received your good things, and likewise Lazarus bad things; but now he is being comforted here, and you are in agony. And besides all this, between us and you there is a great chasm fixed, in order that those who wish to come over from here to you may not be able, and that none may cross over from there to us.' Then he said, 'Then I beg you, father, that you send him to my father's house, for I have five brothers, that he warn them, lest they also come to this place of torment.' But Abraham said, 'They have Moses and the Prophets; let them hear them.' But he said, 'No, Father Abraham, but if someone goes to them from the dead, they will repent!' But he said to him, 'If they do not listen to Moses and the Prophets, neither will they be persuaded if someone rises from the dead.'"

What a story! What a parable of what happens in life and the afterlife! It's such a contrast. It's a contrast between a rich man and a poor man; a contrast between a man who lived in splendor and a man who lived in squalor; a contrast between a man who enjoyed pleasure and delight every day versus a man who experienced pain and degradation every day. But all this gets flipped when they die. The rich man becomes a poor man, and the poor man becomes a rich man. The rich man goes to hell, and the poor man goes to heaven. The rich man is now in pain, and the poor man is now experiencing the pleasures of eternity. The rich man is now in flames, and the poor man is now in comfort.

What does Jesus want us to learn from this story that He told about life and the afterlife? Notice with me three key truths.

Truth number one: Learn the truth regarding earthly success. Jesus gave this parable in direct response to the Pharisees. He is in an uncomfortable situation with them, and He tells this story to open their blind eyes.

Now, in Luke chapter 16, at the beginning of the chapter, He's talking about wealth, and He says this in verse 13, "No servant can serve two masters; for either he will hate the one and love the other, or else he will hold to one and despise the other. You cannot serve God and wealth, God and riches. Now the Pharisees, who were lovers of money, were listening to all these things and they were scoffing at Him." They were rolling their eyes at Him. They were turning up their nose at Him, like, "Oh, what a rube. What a dummy. He doesn't understand this at all. Does He not know that when you are wealthy that shows that you're blessed of God, that you have the favor of God, that you have the approval of God?" They equated money and success with God's approval and God's favor. "And Jesus said to them, 'You are those who justify yourselves in the sight of men, but God knows your hearts, for that which is highly esteemed among men is detestable in the sight of God'" (Luke 16:15).

And then, in just a few verses, He goes into this story about this guy who was so wildly rich. I mean, he would have been on the television show, *Lifestyles of the Rich and Famous.* He had so much, because it says of him, "He habitually dressed in purple and fine linen." Purple is the color of royalty. To make a purple dye, you had to get it from a certain shellfish. It was expensive to produce the dye needed to take the linen and make it purple. Well, that's how this guy dressed. He dressed to the nines every single day. And it says he was gaily living in splendor every day. Every day was a big party. He had so much. This rich man was uber wealthy, far beyond anything the wealthiest Pharisee could even imagine.

And then the contrary was the poor man just dumped at his gate. It said he was "laid at his gate," but that might be better understood as dumped, thrown down, discarded at the rich man's gate like a piece of human garbage. Lazarus, whose name means "Whom the Lord helps," does not seem to be getting much help, does he? He was definitely not getting any help from the rich man. He's covered in sores, which is probably an indication that he was crippled, and he had bed sores. To make matters worse, the dogs would come and lick and gnaw on the sores. You know how dogs do if you get a cut on your leg or something like that. The dog starts licking it, and he starts to kind of nibble at it. It's painful! But that's what dogs do. Furthermore, when Jesus talked about the dogs licking Lazarus' sores, He's not talking about the nice little groomed dog that you have at home that sleeps in your bed at night. These dogs were mongrel dogs, the nasty dogs that would roam the cities and the slums and the back alleys. These are not the dogs you want anywhere near you.

Lastly, no one was giving anything to this poor, crippled, sore-covered man—not even the smallest scrap of food. Jesus said, "(He was) longing to be fed with the crumbs which were falling from the rich man's table." He was longing for it, but not getting it.

So, you have the rich guy, and he's super rich. He has everything this world can offer. You have the poor guy, and he's super poor. He has nothing that this world can offer! Such a contrast between these two men.

The Pharisees said, "Hey, when you have a lot economically and monetarily, that shows that God is blessing you. That shows that God is favoring you. God is approving of you." And so, in this story, when the rich man dies, they would have said, "Well, he's going to be ushered straight into heaven." The poor man, why is he so poor? Why does he have nothing? Why does he just have sores that the dogs are licking? "Well, because he's cursed of God and when he dies, he's going to go to hell." That's in their mind and Jesus is shocking them with His story. Learn the truth regarding earthly success.

Riches are a hurdle to heaven, not proof of assured entrance. Why are riches a hurdle to heaven? Because no man can serve two masters. The default setting for us, especially in today's world here in America, is we worship money. Everything is about money. We make the decisions that we make based on money. We worship money and use God when we're supposed to worship God and use money. Money is amoral. That means it's neither good nor bad. It's not immoral, it's amoral. Your attitude toward money can be moral or immoral. The Scripture says in 1 Timothy, chapter 6, "For the love of money is a root of all sorts of evil. And some by longing for it have wandered away from the faith and pierced themselves with many a pang." The religious leaders, the Pharisees, were "lovers of money" (Luke 16:14). They said, however, that they were lovers of God. And they did not see a contradiction between loving God and loving money. In their way of thinking, money was a good thing, because if you have a lot of money, you have a lot of favor from God. Riches are a sign of God's approval.

The reality, as this parable clearly teaches, is that riches are a hurdle to heaven. You remember the rich young ruler who came to Jesus, asking about inheriting eternal life? He had so much. And Jesus said to him, "You know the commandments." He said, "Yes, and I've kept all those from my youth up." Jesus lovingly responded, "One thing you lack: go and sell all you possess, and give to the poor, and you shall have treasure in heaven; and come, follow Me."

In this important dialogue, Jesus was saying to him, "Here's your real problem, rich young ruler. You have another god other than God, and that other god is money. The way you inherit eternal life is by turning from your false god of wealth and turning to Me. Then you'll have treasure in heaven." And the rich young ruler said, "I can't do that. I don't want to do that. I have far too much to give up." And he went away sad. He was one who owned much property. After that guy walked away, Jesus didn't run after him to try to work out a compromise. He let the man walk away. But He did say to His disciples, "How hard it will be for those who are wealthy to enter the kingdom of God. And the disciples were amazed at His words" (Mark 10:23-24). Why were they amazed? Because they believed like the Pharisees believed. Hey, if you have a lot, that means God is approving of you. On the contrary, Jesus said in effect, "No, when you have a lot, you have to beware, because your wealth can become your god, creating a hurdle to heaven."

Riches are amoral. They are neither good nor bad. You have a lot of wealthy people in the Bible. Abraham was wealthy. Solomon was wealthy. David was wealthy. In the Book of Genesis, Joseph was the number two guy in all of Egypt, and he was wealthy. Lots of people in the scriptures were wealthy. It's okay to have wealth as long as wealth doesn't have you. You see, it is your heart attitude toward riches that makes the difference. When you start to love money, you cease to love God.

Riches are given, and they're to be used to honor God and help men. So, here is this rich guy in the story who has so much, but he's not honoring God by helping his fellow man. Proverbs 3, verse 9 says, "Honor the LORD from your wealth and from the first of all your produce." Honor the Lord with what He gives you. Jesus said this: "Do not lay up for yourselves treasures upon earth where moth and rust destroy, and where thieves break in and steal. But lay up for yourselves treasures in heaven where neither moth nor rust destroys, and where thieves do not break in and steal. For where your treasure is, there will your heart be also." Question: Where's your treasure? If your treasure is all here on planet earth, that's where your heart will be. But if your treasure is in heaven, your heart will be for the things of heaven, and you'll see what really matters—God, His Word, and people coming to a saving knowledge of Jesus.

Now, this rich guy had a great opportunity before him as they dumped Lazarus at his gate. He could feed him. He could doctor his sores. He could clean him up and clothe him. He could treat him as the good Samaritan treated the Jew who fell among robbers. But alas, he didn't lift a finger to provide one iota of assistance. He doesn't even give him a crumb from his table. He doesn't care about him at all.

Now remember this: When it comes to helping people, we are to help those who *cannot* help themselves, not help those who *will not* help themselves. There's a big difference between those. We help those who *cannot* work, not those who *will not* work. We have a lot of people today, a growing number of people today, who are able-bodied and have chosen not to work. We don't help people like that. The Scripture says don't do that. In Second Thessalonians chapter 3, verse 10, Paul told the Thessalonians, "When I was with you, I gave you this order: if a man will not work, neither let him eat." Don't help the guy if he won't help himself. We help those who cannot help themselves. Lazarus could not help himself. He was totally destitute. He was seemingly crippled, and he was covered in sores. He desperately needed help because he was unable to help himself. I love what John Wooden, the legendary coach of the UCLA Bruins once said, "The worst thing you can do for the ones you love is the things they should be doing for themselves." Don't enable people to be slugs, freeloaders, ne'er-do-wells, and those who refuse to work. Don't help those folks. Let them go hungry. Hunger is a great motivator—just ask the prodigal son.

The poor man in this parable, however, could not help himself. He needed the rich man to help him. But the rich man wouldn't give him the time of day. He would not spare even a crumb. His money and luxurious lifestyle were far more important than helping Lazarus, a Jewish brother, in need. Wealth had so blinded the rich man that he could not remotely see the things God deemed important.

Second truth: Learn the truth regarding life after death. I like how distinctly it is put in verse 22, "And it came about that the poor man died, and he was carried away by the angels to Abraham's bosom; and the rich man also died, and he was buried." The poor man wasn't buried. Why? Because it cost money to bury somebody, and this guy doesn't have anything or anybody. He's just dumped at the gate. And when he dies, they just pick up his body and they dump him in the garbage pit. The rich man most likely had a big funeral. He died and was buried.

Listen! You mark it down: Apart from the return of Christ, everyone dies. I don't care how much money you have. You're not going to cheat death. You're not going to somehow get out of death. Lazarus died, and that was a wakeup call to the rich man. "Hey, what happened to me is happening to you." As that tombstone said, "I'm in eternity and you're on the brink." Lazarus died, and the rich man also died. Death is the great leveler, the great equalizer. Hebrews chapter 9, verse 27 says this: "And inasmuch as it is appointed for men to die once and after this comes judgment." We die once. We don't go through reincarnation. God is not into recycling. And so, you don't get recycled. You die once. And then, what happens? Then comes the judgment. Everyone dies.

First Corinthians 15 says, "Behold, I tell you a mystery. We shall not all sleep, but we shall all be changed in a moment, in the twinkling of an eye, at the last trump. The dead in Christ rise first, and then we who are alive and remain shall be caught up together with them in the clouds to meet the Lord in the air." If Jesus delays His coming, a hundred years from now, everyone reading this book is dead—everyone. You say, "I'm only ten years old." Yeah, how many one hundred-ten-year-old people do you know? I hate to be the bearer of bad news, but a hundred years from now everyone reading this is dead. You say, "Well, that's not very comforting." Maybe not, but it is true. It is reality. It is a brutal fact of life.

I was at a funeral a couple of months ago. It was for an older person, and it was an older crowd. I mentioned that a hundred years from now we'll all be dead. And then I looked around and said, "For some of you, it's not a hundred years, it's more like a hundred days. Good grief, I hope some of you can make it through the weekend!" Death is coming. It's the great equalizer. Everyone dies.

And then, everyone lives eternally in either heaven or hell. Lazarus died, and he was carried away by the angels to Abraham's bosom. And the rich man also died, and it says, "In Hades he lifted up his eyes, being in torment, and saw Abraham far away and Lazarus in his bosom." Now, you can press this to the point where you have places for all these things. I don't know how much in this story you have to press into a neat little theological box and say, "Okay, there's a place in the afterlife called Abraham's bosom." It clearly says this in Luke 16. Jesus could simply be saying that Lazarus went to Abraham's side. He went to where Father Abraham was. He went to a place of great honor. But there could be a particular place in the afterlife, before the resurrection of Jesus, called Abraham's bosom or Paradise (see Luke 23:43). You see, when Old Testament people died, they went to the place of the dead called Sheol. Sheol has two compartments: Abraham's bosom/Paradise and Hades. Old Testament believers could not go to heaven since the price for their salvation had not yet been paid. So, their souls went to a holding place, a place of bliss. The unrighteous dead went to Hades, a place of torment and flames, awaiting the Great White Throne Judgment (see Revelation 20:11-15) and eternal hell.

The word *Hades* is used in the Bible ten times, only in the New Testament. Hell is used in the New Testament thirteen times, almost always from the mouth of Jesus. In twelve of those thirteen references to hell, the Greek word used is *gehenna*. Gehenna was the valley of Gen-Hinnom. That's where the Old Testament Jews sacrificed their babies to the false, detestable god known as Molech. For a time, the people of Israel actually adopted the abominable pagan practice of child sacrifices. When God brought reformation to the land under King Josiah, they turned the Gen-Hinnom, the place of child sacrifices, into a garbage dump where the fire was always burning.

Is there a difference between Hades and hell? They are similar places, but hell is forever. You see, when a person dies without Christ, they go immediately to Hades. Hades is like the county jail. If you commit a crime and get arrested, where do you go? You go to jail. You don't go directly to prison. They take you to jail, because in jail you await your day in court. After your day in court, if you are found to be guilty of a serious crime, your sentence is carried out in prison. Jail and prison are very similar, but they aren't exactly the same. One is more permanent than the other. Hades and hell are similar places, but hell is the place of eternal torment. It is the place "where the worm does not die and the fire is not quenched" (Mark 9:44, 9:46, and 9:48).

Now when Jesus was dying on the cross, He said to the repentant thief, "Truly, I say to you, today you shall be with Me in Paradise," Jesus went to Paradise the moment He breathed His last on the cross. When He got there, He told all the righteous dead who inhabited Paradise, "I am the One that was coming to save you. You believed in God's provision for your sin, and that provision is Me." Furthermore, it says in Ephesians 4:8, "When He ascended on high, He led captive a host of captives." He took all those people who were in Paradise (or Abraham's bosom, if you prefer), and He led them to heaven. See, you can't go to heaven until the Lord dies on the cross and rises again from the dead because He had to pay the price. "Behold, the Lamb of God who takes away the sin of the world." He had to take away the sin of the world. The Scripture says, "It is impossible for the blood of bulls and goats to take away sins" (Hebrews 10:4). So, Jesus had to come, Jesus had to die, and Jesus had to rise from the dead. Abraham's bosom, Paradise, has been taken to heaven. If you die today as a believer in Jesus, you do not go to Paradise. Paul said in 2 Corinthians 5:8, "To be absent from the body and to be at home with the Lord." Learn the truth regarding life after death.

And then, thirdly: Learn the truth regarding hell. The emphasis of this story is not on Abraham's bosom. It's not on Paradise. It's not on heaven. The emphasis is on Hades—and every soul in Hades ends up in eternal hell. They are very similar places and can almost be viewed interchangeably. The rich man gives us a first-person account as to the horrors of hell.

Look at it again in verse 23. It says, "And in Hades he lifted up his eyes, being in torment, and saw Abraham far away and Lazarus in his bosom. And he cried out and said, 'Father Abraham, have mercy on me, and send Lazarus, that he may dip the tip of his finger in water and cool off my tongue, for I am in agony in this flame." What do we learn from the rich man about this terrible, horrible place called Hades/hell?

First of all, hell is a place of torment and agony and fire. Jesus talked about hell more than He talked about heaven. He talked about hell more than any other preacher because He knows hell is a real place—and He doesn't want *anyone* to go there. Jesus called it the fiery hell. He called it the place of unquenchable fire. It's a place of agony, and it's a place of torment. The words agony and torment are both used twice in this parable. This place is far more awful than anything your mind can imagine. Sometimes you hear people mock and laugh at the idea of hell. They say, "You know, I want to go to hell. It's gonna be fun!" I mean, AC/DC sings, *"I'm on the highway to hell; no stop signs, speed limit, nobody's gonna slow me down ... I'm on the way to the promised land."* How sick, twisted, and deceived.

When I was in college, I was told Bon Scott, the lead singer for AC/DC, died by choking on his own vomit during a drunken stupor. He was only thirty-three years old. Well, based on all I can gather from his life, he woke up in a Christless hell. He woke up in torment and flames. I'm very confident he doesn't see hell as the promised land any longer. He seemingly couldn't wait to get there. Now he is there and would give anything to get just a few seconds of relief from hell.

The rich man died and went to Hades/hell. He's in agony in the flame. No more living in splendor. Now all he has is agony and torment. Sometimes you will hear people say, "Well, I want to go to hell, because all my friends will be there. We'll sit around and have a big time. We'll play poker." How many people do you know that play poker in a 2,000-degree blast furnace? You don't play poker in hell. It is not a place of fun and games. It's a place of torment, agony, and flames. Jesus said, "In that place there shall be weeping and gnashing of teeth" (Matthew 13:42).

Secondly: Hell is a place of awareness and remembrance. The rich man knows he's in hell. Now, he's shocked by that reality, but he knows immediately where he is. He's aware of his surroundings. He's aware of the fact that he's in fire. "I'm in agony in this flame, in this blaze." Hell's not a place where you lose all consciousness. Hell's not a place where you go into annihilation. No! In hell, you know where you are, and you know what's going on. It's a place of awareness, and it's a place of remembrance.

Now seeing Lazarus in Abraham's bosom is probably given more for illustration's sake. If you're in Hades, can you really see across the great chasm into Paradise? Can you see Abraham and Lazarus right there next to him? That would seem a little inconsistent with what we know from Scripture concerning life after death. There is no indication that in heaven, we see into hell. But in this story, Jesus said the rich man is having a conversation with Abraham. "Hey, send Lazarus. This is all I ask for. Just a drop of water on my tongue to try and cool it. I'm in agony in this flame." And Abraham says to him, "Child, remember." This guy's a son of Abraham, a descendant of Abraham. Remember the Jews put a lot of stock into that pedigree. They would proudly announce, "We're Abraham's children!" John the Baptist burst their proud bubble when he said to them, "God is able from these stones to raise up children to Abraham" (Matthew

3:9). Just because you're a Jew, that doesn't mean anything. What matters is this: have you put your faith and trust in Jesus Christ, God's only Son and man's only Savior?

Many people today try to play the pedigree card. "Well, my dad is a good Christian. My mom is a good Christian. My grandfather was a pastor." Whoopty doo! Good for them, but what about you? It doesn't matter about your mom, your dad, or your grandfather. It matters about you. Sin is personal and so is salvation. Being related by blood to a true Christian means nothing to God. He has no grandchildren, only children. No one gets to heaven on the coattails of another's faith.

So, Abraham responds in this manner, "Child, you are a descendant of mine, but you don't have faith. And that is a critical omission." He goes on to say, "Child, remember that during your life you received your good things, and likewise Lazarus bad things; but now he's being comforted here, and you are in agony." My father-in-law, Rev. Gerald Canon said, "In hell, you'll remember." "Child, remember …" A person's mind is working in hell. Those in hell remember all the opportunities they squandered, all the times they rejected the gospel, all the times they said an emphatic no to Jesus. They will remember all the times they laughed at hell, scoffed at hell, and made fun of those warning them about hell.

A mom was talking to her son one night. He had just come back from his tour in the armed services. He wasn't a Christian, and she was so burdened for him. As he was getting ready to go out on the town for a big night of drinking and sin, she handed him a gospel tract. He looked at that gospel tract, and he threw it down in anger, saying, "Why are you giving me this? The day I came home and got off the bus somebody handed me one of these tracts. Is there any place that I can go where someone won't give one of these?" With tears in her eyes she said to her son, "In hell, no one will give you a tract." "Child, remember ..." And do you know what's interesting, too, about this story? It's Lazarus and the rich man—who is not given.a name in this story.

Lazarus has a name. Why doesn't the rich man have a name? The theologians give him the name Dives because *dives* is the Latin word for rich. Why doesn't he have a name? Because in hell you don't have a name. You have no relationships in hell. You are alone and in agony in the flame. Hell is a place of awareness and remembrance.

And thirdly: Hell is a place of eternal punishment. It's eternal. It's fixed, because Abraham goes on to say in verse 26, "And besides all this, between us and you there is a great chasm fixed, in order that those who wish to come over from here to you may not be able, and that none may cross over from there to us." Hey, once you die, things are fixed. If you die without Christ, you will end up like the rich man in hell. And you will be there for all eternity. Forever is a long time to get it wrong, a long time to roll the dice on your eternity. The rich man is never getting out of Hades/hell. You see, it is not like rehab. It's not like you will be there for a while and then graduate somehow, by hook or by crook, into heaven. It doesn't work that way. The agony and torment of hell are eternal. If you die without personal faith in Jesus, you breathe your last in this life, and then your forever is fixed. See, we really are on the brink of eternity.

One tombstone had these sobering words etched upon it, *"My friend, as you pass by, as you are now, so once was I. As I am now, so you will be. Prepare, my friend, to follow me."* Somebody wrote a note on that tombstone in reply, *"To follow you is not my intent until I know which way you went."* Hey, where are you going? Because once you breathe your last, it is fixed, and it is eternal. Jesus said this in Mark chapter 9, "And if your hand causes you to stumble, cut it off; it is better for you to enter life crippled than having your two hands to go into hell, into the unquenchable fire, where the worm does not die, and the fire is not quenched." It is forever and ever and ever. It's a horrible place.

And lastly: Hell is a place for all who refuse to listen and repent. That's what it is. This rich man represents all those who refuse to listen, who refuse to repent. He has no faith in God's provision for his sins. He wasn't even thinking about that. He was a lover of money, just like the Pharisees, and he thought that he was going to make it into heaven, and he was shocked that he found himself in hell.

You know what's interesting? George Barna did a survey in 2003, and he found that the vast majority of Americans, over 70%, believe in a literal heaven and hell. Over 70%! That's a big percentage. But here is the astounding part, less than one-half of 1% of Americans think they're going to hell. They believe in hell, but they don't think they're going to hell. Hell is for somebody else. Hell is not for me. Isn't that strange?

In the famous sermon on the mount, Jesus gave this sobering plea, "Enter by the narrow gate; for the gate is wide and the way is broad that leads to destruction, and many are those who enter by it. For the gate is small and the way is narrow that leads to life, and few are those who find it" (Matthew 7:13-14). He went on to say, "Many will say to Me on that day, 'Lord, Lord, did we not prophecy in Your name, and in Your name cast out demons, and in Your name perform many miracles? Then I will declare to them, 'I never knew you; Depart from Me, you who practice lawlessness'" (Matthew 7:22-23). "Many will say to Me on that day …" Not a few, but many! And so, people will be shocked to end up in hell. And why are they there? Is it because God is mean and cruel and capricious and just said, "I don't like you. Get out of My face. You're going to hell?" Certainly not! They will be there because "they did not receive the love of the truth so as to be saved" (2 Thessalonians 2:10). They said no to the cross of Christ.

They insulted the Spirit of grace. They refused to repent and believe. And they will die in their sins.

So, Abraham says to the rich man, "I can't send Lazarus to dip a drop of water from his finger on your tongue. There's a chasm fixed. This is fixed. We can't come across." And verse 27, "Then he says, 'I beg you, Father Abraham, that you send him to my father's house, for I have five brothers, that he may warn them, lest they also come to this place of torment. I don't want them to come to this place. Warn them about this place. Send Lazarus." And Abraham said, "They have Moses and the Prophets. Let them hear them." But he said, "No!" The word "no" here is an intensive in the Greek. It's not just a regular no. It's like, "No, no, no, no, Father! If someone goes to them from the dead, they will repent." He's arguing with Abraham. And Abraham says, "If they do not listen to Moses and the Prophets, neither will they be persuaded if someone rises from the dead."

Jesus rose from the dead. How did the religious leaders respond to that news that they got from the soldiers who were guarding the tomb? "Here's some money. You say His disciples stole away the body." That was a blatant lie; and all of them knew it was a lie. But they chose a lie over the truth. And they persecuted those who preached the resurrection of Jesus.

How about another Lazarus in John chapter 11? Jesus raises him from the dead. Well, that's amazing. Everybody should believe now. Lazarus (He whom God helps) has been raised from the dead. How do the Jewish religious leaders respond to this undeniable miracle? Surely they responded in repentance and faith, right? Wrong! Their answer to this tremendous miracle was to plot to kill both Jesus and Lazarus—Jesus for doing the miracle and Lazarus for being the evidence. Unbelievable!

What Abraham said to the rich man was exactly right. "If they won't listen to Moses and the Prophets, if they won't listen to the Word of God, you're not going to convince them even if you show them a miracle." Jesus showed the Pharisees and the religious leaders miracle after miracle after miracle after miracle. They couldn't deny the miracles, so what did they do? "How do we explain this? This guy is doing all this stuff. How can we possibly explain this? I know. He casts out demons by Beelzebul, the ruler of the demons (see Matthew 12:22-32). His power comes from hell." That was their conclusion. Miracles don't make people believe. People have to respond to the Word of God to believe. They have to see that they are sinners in desperate need of a Savior, and cry out with blind Bartimaeus, "Jesus, Son of David, have mercy on me."

Now, there are two words in this man's soliloquy from hell that really jump out. He says in verse 28, "Father Abraham, I have five brothers. Send Lazarus, that he may warn them, lest they come to this place of torment. I want my brothers to be warned. I don't want them to come here. I wouldn't wish this on my worst enemy. Warn them!" As I was studying this, those two words, "Warn them," just leaped into my heart. That's my job and your job—to warn people of the wrath that is to come. That's what John the Baptist said to the religious leaders, "Who warned you to flee from the wrath that is to come?" We warn people, "This is what is happening. If you reject Christ, this is where you're going to end up." And He doesn't want you to be there, and I don't want you to be there. If a man, a woman, a boy or girl ends up in hell, they have to trip over the cross of Christ to get there. He's "not willing for any to perish, but for all to come to repentance" (2 Peter 3:9). He "desires all men to be saved and come to the knowledge of the truth" (1 Timothy 2:4).

But if you blow Him off, hell is where you go. And so, we warn people, and we pray for people. You have people in your family that aren't believers? They're one heartbeat away from eternal hell, to be in agony in this flame day after day after day after day. There's no hope in hell. As Bernard Baruch once said, "Across the portals of hell are written these words: "Abandon all hope, ye who enter here." There is never a good day in hell. Every day is horrible, and there's no hope of ever getting out. "Warn them to not come to this place." And he says, "Warn them, so that they will repent." Verse 30, "Father Abraham, but if someone goes to them from the dead, they will repent." Repentance is key. Jesus said, "Unless you repent, you will all likewise perish." He said that in Luke chapter 13, verse 3. You say, "Well, I would need it more than once." He says it again in Luke chapter 13, verse 5, "I tell you, no, but unless you repent, you will all likewise perish." The apostle Paul preached "repentance toward God and faith in our Lord Jesus Christ" (Acts 20:21). Those two things are critical. You can't get saved without repentance. That is why when people try to attach their sin, and say, "Well, I'm this kind of a Christian. I'm this sinning kind of a Christian. This is part of me. This is who I am," you can't get saved like that. You have to repent of sin. You have to turn from sin. You don't bring your sin to the Lord, and say, "Well, Lord, You're going to have to accept me and my sin." He said, "I'll never do that. I hate sin. I can't have fellowship with sin. My eyes are too pure to look upon sin," as it says in the Book of Habakkuk. "So, if you will turn from your sin, I will save you. If you hold onto your sin, you will die in your sins. Unless you repent, you will all likewise perish." That's straight Scripture.

Hey, listen! I didn't write this story. I didn't make up this story. I'm reading to you, "Thus says the Lord." If this parable from Jesus makes you mad, take it up with God. Some people say, "Well, I don't believe in a God who would send anyone to hell." God doesn't send you to hell. You send yourself to hell. He's done everything to keep you from hell. You don't have to shake your fist in the face of God and say, "I'll never believe in You." All you have to do is just say, "That's nice." You just say with the Doobie Brothers, *"Jesus is just alright with me."* I'm going to keep doing my own thing. And then, one day you will die, and you will find yourself in hell forever.

I was privileged to be a part of the funeral service for Bobby Choate, a great member of our church for many, many years. I shared this poem at his service. You know, the thing about funerals, you can talk to people at funerals about their soul, because they come thinking about death. They can't avoid the subject at a funeral. And as the Scripture says in Ecclesiastes 7, "The day of one's death is better than the day of one's birth; It is better to go to a house of mourning than to go to a house of feasting ..." Why? "... Because that is the end of every man, and the living takes it to heart."

Everybody must face the reality of death. Lazarus died, the rich man died, and you and I will die one day, too. The poem I shared at Bobby's funeral is titled, *"Five Minutes After I Die."*

> "Loved ones will weep o'er my silent face,
> Dear ones will clasp me in sad embrace,
> Shadows and darkness will fill the place,
> Five minutes after I die.
>
> But faces that sorrow I will not see,

Voices that murmur, they will not reach me,

But where, O where will my spirit be,

Five minutes after I die.

Not to repair the good I lack,

Fixed to the goal of my chosen track,

No room to repent, no turning back,

Five minutes after I die.

Mated forever with my chosen throng,

Long is eternity, O so long.

Then woe is me if my soul be wrong,

Five minutes after I die."

Jesus doesn't want anyone to go to hell. He died for you on the cross. And if you will put your faith where God put your sins, on the Lord Jesus Christ, you can be saved today. You can know that you know that you know that you know that you've been born again and that you're on the highway to heaven. And five minutes after you die, you're going to be experiencing the glories of heaven. That is what is in store for every child of God. It's the decision you make in this life that determines eternity. If you don't know Jesus, today is the day for you.

CHAPTER TWO

From Savior to Judge

And I saw the dead, the great and the small, standing before the throne, and books were opened; and another book was opened, which is the book of life; and the dead were judged from the things which were written in the books, according to their deeds. Revelation 20:12

Robert Ingersoll was a man who lived in the 1800s. His father was a pastor, but Ingersoll rejected the faith. He was a lawyer. He was a writer. He was an orator. He was known as the great agnostic. He was speaking one day to a crowd of people on this subject: *The Absurdity of Hell.* And he told the crowd that he was going to prove to them, beyond any shadow of a doubt, that hell did not exist. A half-drunken man in the crowd yelled out, "Make your argument strong, Bob. There are a lot of us poor fellows depending on you. If you are wrong, we are sunk!"

You know, when we try and wrap our minds around eternity, we can't do it. It's just unfathomable. And when we try and wrap our minds around heaven, we can't do it. The Bible says in 1 Corinthians 2:9, "THINGS WHICH EYE HAS NOT SEEN AND EAR HAS NOT HEARD, AND which HAVE NOT ENTERED THE HEART OF MAN, ALL THAT GOD HAS PREPARED FOR THOSE WHO LOVE HIM." Heaven is so much greater than our minds can comprehend. And hell is so much worse than our minds can comprehend. Heaven is an eternal reality, and so is hell.

Now, many are like Robert Ingersoll. We want to argue away hell and say it doesn't exist. There are even those who are Christians and who preach the Word of God that want to say, "No, hell does not exist. It's not a real place." One man was speaking at a conference, a Christian conference in Edinburgh, and he said this: "I believe that endless torture is a hideous and unscriptural doctrine, which has been a terrible burden on the mind of the church for many centuries, and a terrible blot on her presentation of the gospel. I should indeed be happy before I die if I could help in sweeping it away." You can't sweep it away. You can't explain it away. You can't argue it away. It's in the Word of God. And just as heaven is a real place, and people will spend eternity there who trusted Christ, hell is also a real place, and people will spend eternity there who rejected Christ. So, what does the Bible have to say about those who do not put their faith and trust in Christ, or as Old Testament people, did not put their faith and trust in God's provision for their sin? You see, with Old Testament people, they didn't know the name of Jesus. Jesus hadn't come yet. They were saved by putting their faith and trust in God's provision for their sin. We're saved in New

Testament times by putting our faith and trust in God's provision for our sin, and we know that God's provision for our sin is His Son, the Lord Jesus Christ, as He died upon the cross.

When the apostle Paul was being tried by Felix at Caesarea-by-the-Sea, he said these words: "There shall certainly be a resurrection of both the righteous and the wicked" (Acts 24:15). In this chapter, we're going to look at the resurrection of the wicked, because you mark it down: there will certainly be a resurrection of the wicked— and that comes at the end of time. The Bible talks about it in Revelation chapter 20.

So, just to give you a frame of reference, when is this time coming? The Bible calls this horrible event the Great White Throne Judgment, the final judgment, the last judgment. It is the end of time before eternity begins. We have a little graph to help you see where things are.

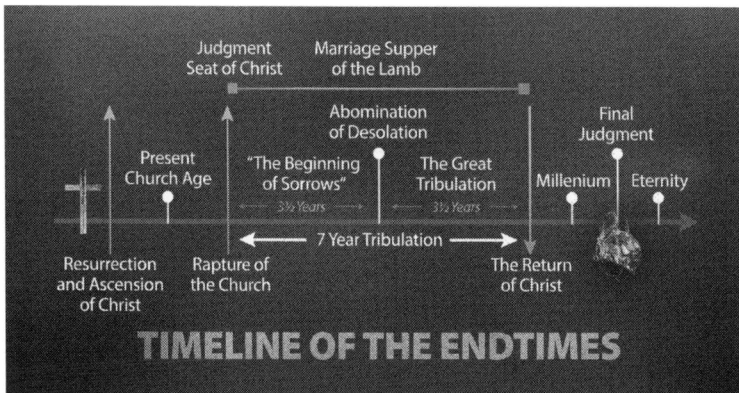

TIMELINE OF THE ENDTIMES

Right now, we're in the present Church Age. That's the time that we're living. It's the time between the cross/resurrection and the rapture of the church. That's the Church Age. And we believe that the rapture of the church is coming. It's a signless event. It could come at any moment. Jesus said, "An hour when you think not, the Son of Man comes." And when the rapture of the church takes place, then we have the years of tribulation, the seven years of tribulation that are spoken of in Daniel chapter 9. The last half of that tribulation is the worst. It's called the Great Tribulation. At the desecration of the temple, that middle point, that's when the Antichrist, who is the devil in the flesh, reveals his true colors. He says, "No more worship of God. I am God. You worship me. And if you don't worship me, you will be killed." That declaration (called the abomination of desolation as the abominable one, the Antichrist, makes the temple desolate and detestable) sets up the Great Tribulation. Jesus Christ comes back to this earth at the battle of Armageddon and does battle with the Antichrist and all his forces. He defeats them with the sharp sword that comes out of His mouth—the power of His word. Then He sets up His kingdom in Jerusalem. There will be a time period of a thousand years where the Lord

Jesus Christ will reign in person on this earth, along with His glorified saints. We who were raptured and martyred will rule and reign with Him. And at the end of the millennial reign of Christ, there is the Great White Throne Judgment. It's the final judgment before the eternal state. In the eternal state, everything is fixed. No babies are being born. Every soul ever created is either judged and in hell or glorified and in heaven. And there's a new heaven and a new earth. You can read about the eternal state in Revelation chapters 21 and 22.

So, let's look at the final judgment, the Great White Throne Judgment, spoken of in Revelation chapter 20, beginning in verse 11:

> And I saw a great white throne and Him who sat upon it, from whose presence earth and heaven fled away, and no place was found for them. And I saw the dead, the great and the small, standing before the throne, and books were opened; and another book was opened, which is the book of life; and the dead were judged from the things which were written in the books, according to their deeds. And the sea gave up the dead which were in it, and death

and Hades gave up the dead which were in them, and they were judged, every one of them according to their deeds. And death and Hades were thrown into the lake of fire. This is the second death, the lake of fire. And if anyone's name was not found written in the book of life, he was thrown into the lake of fire.

Paul said there will certainly be a resurrection of the wicked. The resurrection of the wicked takes place right here at the Great White Throne Judgment. Since there is certainly going to be a resurrection of the wicked, I want to share with you three certainties that we see from the Great White Throne Judgment.

Certainty number one: The Judge will sit on His great white throne. Sometimes, confused people will pray something like this, "Lord, I can't wait to meet You at Your great white throne." You don't want to meet the Lord at the great white throne. That's a judgment of all unbelievers. "And I saw a great white throne and Him who sat upon it, from whose presence earth and heaven fled away, and no place was found for them."

The Judge sits on the throne, and this Judge is terrifying in holiness. He is absolutely terrifying in holiness. I mean, earth and heaven say, "I've got to get out of here." As one translation says, "Earth and sky ran away from Him and disappeared." They said, "We got to get out of here." They run away, and they disappear. Why? Because this is the end of time. No more earth. No more sky. It is done! And this says that there's nowhere to run and nowhere to hide because earth and heaven have fled. In Revelation chapter 6, the people cry out and say to the rocks and the mountains, "Fall on us and hide us from the presence of the Lord, for the day of His wrath has come, and who is able to stand?" You can't cry out to the rocks and mountains at the Great White Throne Judgment because they're gone. This is just an unbeliever before God. It's a terrifying thing. The Bible says, "It is a terrifying thing to fall into the hands of the living God" (Hebrews 10:31). The Bible says, "Our God is a consuming fire" (Hebrews 12:29). Make no mistake. At this final judgment, the Judge will be terrifying in holiness.

And the Judge is none other than the Lord Jesus Christ Himself. From Savior to Judge! Now, we know that God is the Judge. God is the Judge of all the earth. But

Jesus said in John chapter 5:22-23, "For not even the Father judges anyone, but has given all judgment to the Son, in order that all may honor the Son, even as they honor the Father." So, God is going to judge the world in righteousness, but He does it through a man whom He has appointed—and that man is Jesus. That is exactly what Paul told the Athenians on Mars Hill in Acts 17. You know, all the Greek wise men and learned big shots had gotten together to hear what Paul had to say about this Jesus. Paul began to preach to them, and he said, "God is now declaring that all men everywhere should repent, because He has fixed a day in which He will judge the world in righteousness through a man whom He has appointed, having furnished proof to all men by raising Him from the dead" (Acts 17:30-31). The Lord Jesus will sit on the throne. He will be the Judge. The Savior who wanted to save every single person is now the Judge who will judge every single person. Great means that it is great in power and in awesomeness. White means it's great in purity. Throne means its purpose. What is its purpose? To judge in righteousness. So, the Judge will sit on His great white throne.

Second certainty: The judged will be raised to stand trial before Him. You see the Judge. Now we see the judged. It says in verse 12, "And I saw the dead, the great and the small, standing before the throne ..." It says in verse 13, "And the sea gave up the dead which were in it, and death and Hades gave up the dead which were in them ..." There is a resurrection of the wicked.

Now, when a person dies outside of Christ, what happens to that person? Well, as we saw in the previous chapter on Luke 16, when the rich man died, he went to a place called Hades. That's where his soul went. His body went into the ground. The Scripture says, "... he was buried, and in Hades he lifted up his eyes, being in torment." So, the body goes into the grave. The body goes into the crematorium. The body goes into the sea, or wherever you plant the body, but the soul goes to a place called Hades.

Now remember the difference between Hades and hell. Hades is like county jail, and hell is the state penitentiary. No one gets picked up for a crime by a police officer and gets taken right to the state penitentiary. No! He or she is taken to jail. And from jail, the perpetrator stands before the judge. If found guilty of the stated crime, the judge then sentences the offender to the state penitentiary. Hades is the place that all the unrighteous dead go as they await the Great White Throne Judgment. And Hades is similar to hell in that it is a place of torment—but it's only for the soul. The body is in the grave. "But the sea gave up the dead which were in them, and death and Hades gave up the dead which were in them ..." At the great white throne, there is a reuniting of the soul and the body. God gives every wicked person a new body, so to speak, a body that can last forever, a body that will experience the horrors of hell forever and ever and ever. It's not a glorified body like believers get, but it is a body that will last forever. Jesus said, "And do not fear those who kill the body, but are unable to kill the soul; but rather fear Him who is able to destroy both soul and body in hell" (Matthew 10:28).

The judged will be raised to stand trial before Him. And the Scripture says in Revelation 20:12, "And I saw the dead, the great and the small ..." So, who's going to be there at this judgment? Well, it's all the unbelievers of all the ages. See, we have this erroneous idea that when you die, you're going to stand before God to be judged and to determine your eternal destiny, heaven or hell. We erroneously think that God has this big balance, like a chemistry class scale. And God's going to pile all your good works on one side of the scale and all your bad works on the other side of the scale. We think he is going to "weigh us in the balance." Do you remember the children's classic movie, *Willy Wonka and the Chocolate Factory*? There was a scene in that movie with a scale in the chocolate factory that was used to determine good eggs from bad eggs. That's the way people think when it comes to the judgment of God. But it is nothing like that at all. The only people who appear at the Great White Throne Judgment are unbelievers, guilty sinners—bad eggs, if you will. And the only thing that's being decided at this judgment is the degree of punishment.

The judged will be raised to stand trial. So, you have the great and the small, they're going to be there. See, it's from one end of the spectrum to the other. The great are the *megas*. That's the Greek word for great, *megas*. And the small are the *mikro*. We get micro from that. So, you have the big shots and the little shots and all the other shots in between. The great and the small, they're all going to be there.

Sometimes we see evil crimes committed by famous, wealthy, well-connected people. This person can be guilty as sin with overwhelming evidence against them, but somehow, some way, they are found to be innocent. We say, "What in the world?" Just because they have money, just because they have fame, just because they have connections, they can commit an obvious crime and get off with no consequences? What gives? Where is the justice? Well, at the great white throne, no one gets off on a technicality, a legal loophole. The Judge cannot be bribed, bullied, or threatened. In this courtroom, justice will be served. And the great aren't going to be able to finagle their way out of it.

But not only do you have the great and the small, you have the rejecters and the neglecters. You say, "What is that?" Well, it's two ends of the unbelieving spectrum. See, the rejecters are those who are out-and-out against the Lord. They're the Robert Ingersolls of the world. They're the ones who go on speaking tours saying that God doesn't exist. They're the people who hate God, who shake their fist in the face of God, and say, "God, I will never believe in You. I'll never come to faith in You."

There's a poem that I heard years and years ago. I've never forgotten it. It's a godless, Communist poem: "I fight alone, and win or sink, I need no one to make me free. I want no Jesus Christ to think that He could die for me." That's the out-and-out rejecter, shaking his or her puny little fist in the face of God in anger and hatred.

But now, on the other end of the spectrum, what do you have? You have the neglecter. This is not the person who's shaking his/her fist in the face of God. This is not the person that says, "God, I hate You, and I'm never going to believe in You." This is the person who simply neglects and ignores the Lord. Isaiah 53:6 tells us, "All of us like sheep have gone astray, each of us has turned to his own way."

The neglecter is the person who sings the Doobie Brothers famous song, "Jesus Is Just Alright With Me." They say, "I have no beef with Jesus, but I'm going to go do my own thing. I'm not mad at Him. I don't hate Him. I'm just not really going to follow Him. I'm going to do what I want to do."

I can identify with the neglecter because that's what I was as an unsaved high school kid. I wasn't hating God. I just wanted to do my own thing. I didn't understand God and His grace. I was wandering away from Him, chasing thrills and chills, girls and a good time. Now, I always wanted to go to heaven. I just didn't know how to get there. Neglecters are like that. They think, "Well, I'm just kind of doing my own thing. I'm following the crowd. Everybody's doing it, doing it, doing it. I'm just going to go along with them." These neglecters will be at the great white throne.

And then you have the riotous and the religious. They're going to be there. Two ends of the spectrum. What does it mean to be riotous? It means one is wild with uncontrolled and violent behavior. The riotous are living for sin and self, pleasures and possessions. If anyone gets in their way, they won't think twice about ending their life. The riotous are over the top sinners. They will be at the great white throne.

Now, our minds can wrap around that type of sinner being judged. A 2015 Pew Research survey revealed that 58% of people in America believe in hell. That's a sizeable percentage. The only problem is less than ½ of 1% believe they're in danger of going to hell. Hell is always for somebody else. It's for the "bad person." It's for that riotous person. It's for that person shaking his or her fist in the face of God. Hell is for the Adolf Hitlers of the world.

Now, if you mention Hitler's name as Hitler going to hell, nobody seems to get too upset about that. Some may even think hell is too good for a mass murderer like Hitler. Will Hitler spend eternity in hell? Yes. How can I be so sure? Jesus said, "You will know them by their fruits" (Matthew 7:16). Multitudes of evil men and women from history will be there. All who lived riotously and never repented will end up in hell.

But then you have the other side of the spectrum, the religious. The religious person is going to be there. See, this is all under the heading of, "And I saw the dead, the great and the small ..." The rejecters and the neglecters, the riotous and the religious, they will be there. There are a lot of people who are very religious in false religion. And what do they say? "Well, you know, all roads lead to heaven." No, they don't. Only one road leads to heaven, and Jesus said, "I am the way, and the truth, and the life; and no one comes to the Father but through Me" (John 14:6). Those who were religious with world religions will find out that they were terribly deceived.

Even more horrifying is the fact that those who are religious in Judaism and Christianity will be at this judgment also. Caiaphas, who was high priest, who presided over the trial of Jesus, he will be there at the great white throne. His father-in-law, Annas, will be there at the great white throne. All those guys that were part of the religious hierarchy in first century Israel who chose the Law over Jesus, they'll be there. False cultists will be there, along with false prophets and false Christs.

And do you know who else will be there? The person who came to church Sunday after Sunday after Sunday. The person who walked down the aisle at the altar call, who joined the church, who got baptized … the one who checked all the religious boxes but never truly gave his/her heart to Christ will be at the judgment. This is the person who intellectually believed in Jesus, but who never surrendered his/her heart to the Master. In Matthew 7:21-23, Jesus said, "Not everyone who says to Me, 'Lord, Lord,' will enter the kingdom of heaven, but he who does the will of My Father who is in heaven. Many will say to Me on that day (many! Not a few, not some–many!), 'Lord, Lord, did we not prophesy in Your name, and in Your name cast out demons, and in Your name perform many miracles?' Then I will declare to them, 'I never knew you. DEPART FROM ME, YOU WHO PRACTICE LAWLESSNESS.'' What a frightening passage of Scripture. He's not talking about Sunday morning benchwarmers. He's not talking about somebody that says, "Well, Lord, I came at Easter and Christmas. That's got to be good for something." He's talking about the people who preached in His name, who cast out demons in His name, who performed miracles in His name. But they did not know the Lord heart to heart. They never truly believed. They will stand with the condemned at the Judgment Seat of Christ.

And certainty number three: The judgment will be righteously and fairly delivered. "And I saw the dead, the great and the small, standing before the throne, and books were opened; and another book was opened, which is the book of life; and the dead were judged from the things which were written in the books, according to their deeds. The sea gave up the dead which were in it, and death and Hades gave up the dead which were in them, and they were judged, every one of them according to their deeds." How does God judge? He judges righteously. He judges fairly.

The rhetorical question of Genesis 18 reminds us, "Shall not the Judge of all the earth deal justly?"

Remember this about God: He is holy, holy, holy. God is too pure to look upon sin. God will never do judges anything that would be constituted as sin, as unjust. And God is going to judge through the Lord Jesus Christ, He's going to judge righteously and fairly. And so, what's this judgment going to be—because no one who's at the Great White Throne Judgment is going to be acquitted? Everyone is going to be condemned. That's why they are there, because they rejected or neglected Christ. So, the judgment will be based on deeds. They're judged every one of them according to their deeds. God repeats that phrase, "according to their deeds," so that no one misses this important fact.

Now, God has books. Books were opened, and they're judged from the things which are written in the books. You say, "What does that mean?" It means that God is writing down everything we do. He knows everything we say, everything we do, everything we think, every impure thought, every impure motive. God knows it all! David said, "Even before there's a word on my tongue, behold, O

LORD, You know it all" (Psalm 139:4). God records it all. And here is the lost person, and he's raised up, the resurrection of the wicked, and he stands before the Lord Jesus Christ, who has gone from Savior to Judge, and he hears the terrifying, shameful record of his life.

You know what's so ironic about this? See, when you ask the average person, "Hey, if you were to die, do you think you'd go to heaven?" "Oh yeah, probably." You know, it's less than ½ of 1% think they're going to hell. "So, I'll probably go to heaven. Maybe I will have to go to Purgatory for a while, but I will eventually end up in heaven." News Flash! Purgatory doesn't exist. Purgatory is made up. There is no Purgatory in the Bible. There is only eternal heaven or eternal hell. So, this person says, "Well, you know, I guess I'll go to heaven. I'm not 100% confident, but I am fairly confident." "Well, what would you say to God if He said to you, 'Why should I let you into heaven,' what would you say?" "Well, Lord, I'm a pretty good person. Lord, I do some good things." As one man told me, "I've had six kids!" Okay, thumbs up for you, guy, but that doesn't get you into heaven. I asked one guy that question one time. He said, "Well, my brother's a priest." Good for your brother, but what does that have to do with you? We always think in terms of, "Well, I did this good thing, and I did that good thing—and one day I put a few dollars in the offering plate." We have these lists of good things that we have done. Do not miss the tragic irony do with you?" We always think in terms of, "Well, I did this here. Everyone at the great white throne is judged "according to their deeds."

God has a book of all our sins. For the Christian, every sin is paid in full by the blood of Jesus. But for the unbeliever, every sin is still on the books, active and demanding payment. If you find yourself at the Great White Throne Judgment, you will stand there terrified and horrified as every dark and dastardly sin becomes visible in the light of His holiness.

In 1992, I won a sales contest with Nalco Chemical Company. Debbie and I were given an all-expense paid trip to Las Vegas, Nevada. (If you've ever been there, I don't recommend it. You could lose everything you hold dear inside of thirty minutes!) We were initially blown away by the enormous and elaborate hotels. They're huge and over-the-top nice. Well, we were at the Luxor Hotel lobby where they had this photograph booth. They were taking pictures of couples and superimposing their faces on magazine covers which you could buy for $20. We were watching the large TV monitors as couple after couple signed up to have their picture made. What caught my attention were the extremely bright lights they used to capture the face so they could superimpose it onto the magazine cover. The bright lights revealed every blot, blemish, and scar. Regardless of how much make-up one might have had on, nothing was hidden from the penetrating lights. Beautiful women had all their facial imperfections exposed under the lights. There was no escape.

Can you imagine standing before the thrice-holy God of the universe at the Great White Throne Judgment and have every imperfection come to the light? You may have thought you were very moral and upright, but when the light of holiness shines upon you, you will see just how utterly sinful you actually were. It will be horrifying. The judgment will be based on deeds. So much sin. So much punishment. There is no mercy, only pure, unadulterated justice.

Secondly: The judgment will be based on light rejected. How does God judge? Well, He takes into account how much witness you have had. See, hell is not the same for every single person. Heaven is not the same for every single person, either. There are those who get rewarded greatly—as we're going to talk about in the next chapter, the Bema Judgment, the Judgment Seat of Christ—and those who are saved yet so as through fire with no reward. In hell, you have some people, the Adolph Hitler types, for example, who have to account for lots and lots and lots of sins and atrocities. And some others will have much less. This is what Jesus said in Luke chapter 12, "And that slave who knew his master's will and did not get ready or act in accord with his will, shall receive many lashes. But the one who did not know it, and committed deeds worthy of a flogging, will receive but few. And from everyone who has been given much, shall much be required; and to whom they entrusted much, of him they will ask all the more." Do you know what that communicates to you and me? You know where is a dangerous place to be? Church! If you're not going to give your heart to Christ, church is a dangerous place to be. Why? Because you're hearing truth, and you're being given much, and much shall be required.

My brother Larry was an attorney for many, many years. He's retired now. He's a really smart guy. I have always looked up to Larry. He's my oldest sibling. When I got called in the ministry, my brother Larry was very interested in this call. He saw me leave my job and go to the ministry, and he was intrigued by that bold move. When I began to preach on a regular basis, I started sending tapes to my learned brother Larry to critique my content and delivery. Although Larry was pretty much an agnostic at the time, he was willing to listen and critique me. So, he began to listen to sermon after sermon in his car while he commuted to and from work in Houston, Texas traffic.

After a couple of years of this arrangement, I said to him, "Larry, I'm getting concerned about you." He said, "Why is that?" I said, "Because you're hearing lots of truth. And if you don't respond to the truth, all the listening of these sermons is just going to amass judgment against you." You see a person is judged not just by sins committed, but by light rejected. And the good news of that story is, my brother Larry said, "Well, I did respond." And I said, "You did?" He said, "Yeah, about six months ago. And I want to thank you for helping me." I was blown away, and said, "Wow! That is such great news! I have been praying for you for twenty years! I thought you might have let me know when it happened!" I had the privilege of baptizing my brother back in 2002. It was an awesome experience. But see, when you hear truth and don't respond to it, you amass judgment. To whom much has been given, amass judgment. To whom much has been given, shall much also be required. The judgment will be based on light rejected.

People say, "Well, what about the person who's never heard?" Romans chapter 1 tells us about the person who has never heard. This one cannot plead innocence because of ignorance. He has the witness of conscience and the witness of creation, and he is without excuse. "Shall not the Judge of all the earth deal justly?" God will not do anything that won't be just and fair and right and equitable. And remember this, too, about God: He knows the end from the beginning. God knows everything that you do and anything and everything that you would do, given the opportunity, because He can see all scenarios played out. And so, God doesn't have to necessarily see what you did do with a given situation, and say, "Well, I'm judging you based on that." He can judge you based on your heart. He can judge you based on, "Well, I know if you had been given these opportunities, this is how you would have responded." And it will be true, and it will be right, and it will be just. So, the judgment is based on deeds and on light rejected.

And the judgment will be eternal hell. Verse 14 reads, "And death and Hades were thrown into the lake of fire. This is the second death, the lake of fire. And if anyone's name was not found written in the book of life, he was thrown into the lake of fire." That's how the Bible describes hell. It's a lake that burns with fire and brimstone. Now, is hell literal fire? I don't know. That's how it's described. It might be different from literal fire as we know it, but fire is how the Bible describes it. That's what the rich man said in Luke 16, "I am in agony in this flame." There are different ways that Jesus described hell. He said it's the unquenchable fire. He said it's a place of outer darkness. He said it's a place of weeping and wailing and gnashing of teeth. It's a horrible place, beyond anything our mind can fathom. An eternity of people weeping and wailing and gnashing their teeth. You say, "What does it mean to gnash your teeth?" That is what they did when they stoned Stephen when he was preaching a message they hated. He said in Acts 7, "You stiff-necked Jews, always resisting the

Holy Spirit." They got so angry. They were cut to the heart. And they covered their ears and gnashed their teeth at him. That is what a dog does when he gets annoyed. He growls and gnashes his teeth together in anger and retaliation. That's what's going on in hell. People are angry at God. They're blaming God for their situation. They never get out of hell because they all continue to sin as they stew in their hatred toward God.

In the Book of Revelation, when the Lord sends the plague of hailstones down upon men, hundred pounds in weight (see Revelation 16), the people gnaw their tongues in pain and blaspheme God. They do not repent and give Him glory. They refuse to tap out, to use MMA language, and surrender. They just get more and more angry at God, gnashing their teeth at Him in pain, hatred, and uncontrolled rage.

But this is what is so amazing about the Great White Throne Judgment: It could have been avoided! That's right. No one had to be there! "The books were opened, and another book was opened, which is the book of life." Now, no one there at the Great White Throne Judgment has his/her name in the book of life, but the book of life is still opened. Now, why would God open the book of life in the sight of each condemned sinner knowing none of their names are written in there? I believe it is for one main reason—to show each one of them that their name could have been included. Jesus died for every single sinner who has ever been created. First John chapter 2, verses 1-2, "I'm writing these things to you so that you may not sin. And if anyone sins, we have an advocate with the Father, Jesus Christ the righteous. And He Himself is the propitiation for our sins; and not for ours only, but also for those of the whole world." He died for everyone. And the book of life is open. And the Lord shows every doomed sinner that his/her name could have been in the book. Jesus had a place for their name. He shed His blood for them, but they rejected Him and "trampled underfoot the blood of Christ" (Hebrews 12:29). When a sinner says no to the forgiver and insults the Spirit of grace, all that is left for that sinner is judgment and hell. "And if any man's name was not found written in the book of life, he was thrown into the lake of fire." I believe the Lord says to every person before He is thrown into the lake of fire, "Not My will, but yours be done." See, Jesus really doesn't send anybody to hell. You send yourself to hell because you reject His love. You reject His grace. You reject the cross. You reject, you neglect, you bypass, you just think, *I don't need that.* But the reality is you do. Jesus is "the way, and the truth, and the life; and no man comes to the Father but through (Him)" (John 14:6).

Now, as we bring this chapter to an end, I want you to think about the greatest question ever asked in the Bible. The greatest question ever asked in the Bible was a question from the lips of an unbeliever. It was a question from the lips of a guy who's going to be at the Great White Throne Judgment, a guy who's going to end up in hell forever and ever and ever. His name was Pontius Pilate. And this was his question: "Then, what shall I do with Jesus who is called the Christ?" I want you to think about that question because it's the question of all questions. What will you do? Crown Him or crucify Him? Hail Him or nail Him? Receive Him or reject Him? What will you do with Jesus? Listen! What you do with Jesus in this life determines what He does with you in the next.

If you have never trusted Jesus as Savior and Lord, now is your opportunity to do so. The Bible tells us, "Today, if you hear His voice, harden not your heart.

Behold, now is the day of salvation." You have today to get right with God. Pray a prayer like this one from your heart:

> "Dear God, I'm a sinner, and I can't save myself, and I need Jesus. And I don't want to stand before you at the Great White Throne Judgment condemned. Please forgive me, Jesus. Please come into my life and save me. I turn from my sin and surrender my all to you!"

That is the prayer God longs to answer, the prayer of repentance and faith. And I want to tell you, on the authority of the Word of God, that Jesus Christ will save anybody who comes to Him in humility, brokenness, repentance, and faith. You can be saved today if you leave your sin and come to Jesus. Will you do it?

Let me close by quoting the poignant words from a song by A.B. Simpson, "What will you do with Jesus; neutral you cannot be? One day, your soul will be asking, 'What will He do with Me?'"

CHAPTER THREE

When Heaven is on Your Horizon

*For we must all appear before the judgment seat of Christ,
that each one may be recompensed for his deeds in the
body, according to what he has done, whether good or
bad. 2 Corinthians 5:10*

Many people are familiar with the name C. S. Lewis. C. S. Lewis is considered an intellectual giant of the 20th century. He's one of the most influential writers the world has ever known. C. S. Lewis wrote thirty books, and his books have sold a whopping 200 million copies. That's pretty impressive. I've written a few books, and they've sold a whopping 200 copies. No, I'm just kidding. My mom bought 300. Hey, 200 million book sales is beyond amazing! His book, *Mere Christianity* (originally published in 1952), still sells roughly 100,000 copies annually. Lewis wrote in *Mere Christianity:* "If you read history, you will find that the Christians who did the most for the present world were those who thought most about the next. It is since Christians have largely ceased to think of the other world that they've become so ineffective in this." Isn't that interesting? When heaven is on your horizon, you do lots of good for the kingdom and for people in this life. But when heaven is not on your horizon, when you're *not* thinking about the next world, you don't.

So, let me ask you a question. Is heaven on your mind? Is heaven on your horizon? Do you know for certain that you're going there? For a lot of people, heaven is not on their horizon because they don't know where they're going. They have a big question mark when it comes to the issue of what happens after they die.

The previous two chapters of this book focused on the reality of eternal hell and how horrible and awful that is. God doesn't want anyone to go to hell. Hell was not created for people. Jesus said hell was "prepared for the devil and his angels" (Matthew 25:41). He doesn't want people to go there. He's "not wishing for any to perish, but for all to come to repentance" (2 Peter 3:9). We have seen what happens to those who reject and ignore the gospel of our Lord Jesus Christ. When people choose their sin over God's Son, they end up at the Great White Throne Judgment. From there, they are cast into hell, the lake that burns with fire and brimstone.

Now we want to shift gears and look at the eternal reality of heaven. It's so much more pleasant to talk about heaven than it is to talk about hell. Just as hell is far worse than our minds can imagine, heaven is far better. The Bible tells us in 1 Corinthians 2:9, "… but just as it is written, "THINGS WHICH EYE HAS NOT SEEN AND EAR HAS NOT HEARD, AND which HAVE NOT ENTERED

THE HEART OF MAN, ALL THAT GOD HAS PREPARED FOR THOSE WHO LOVE HIM."

The first time I went on a mission trip it was to Acapulco, Mexico. I was in college, and a bunch of us went with our college group from church. I didn't know very much Spanish, and I still don't, but I learned some phrases to be able to share Christ with the locals. There were three questions that I learned in Spanish. The first question: Hacer usted Jesus el Cristo? That means "Do you know Jesus Christ?" And then, the follow-up was: En tu corazon? "In your heart?" "Do you know Jesus Christ—in your heart?" And the third question was this: Seguro? "Are you sure? Are you sure that you know Jesus Christ in your heart?" I still remember one man who was so excited that I asked him that question. He said to me, "True Cristiano!" He knew Jesus in a real saving way. He knew Jesus in his heart.

The big question for you as you read this: do you know Jesus in your heart? Are you certain that you are His, certain that your final destination is heaven?

The apostle Paul sure was, and he lived with heaven on the horizon. He lived with his mind on heaven. He said to the believers in Philippi that he had "the desire to depart and be with Christ, for that is very much better" (Philippians 1:23). We would say amen to that statement. It is very much better to depart and be with Christ.

In Second Corinthians, Paul defends his apostleship, and he gives information to the Corinthians that they desperately need to know. He had talked to them in the Book of First Corinthians about the resurrection. And, he said, "If Christ is not raised, then you're still in your sins." Jesus had to come out of the grave physically, bodily, for your salvation to be valid; for God to put His stamp of approval on the Son's sacrifice on the cross. Without the bodily resurrection of Jesus, there is no forgiveness. And so, Jesus came up from the grave. Paul said to the Corinthians, "Hey, you're going to come up out of the grave one day, too. We shall not all sleep, but we shall all be changed in a moment, in the twinkling of an eye, at the last trumpet, for the dead in Christ shall rise, and, and we will be caught up to be with them in the clouds." He said that in First Corinthians 15. He said it in First Thessalonians chapter 4, also. And he talks about it here in 2 Corinthians.

In 4:16 – 5:10, Paul says, "Therefore we do not lose heart, but though our outer man is decaying, yet our inner man is being renewed day by day. For momentary, light affliction is producing for us an eternal weight of glory far beyond all comparison, while we look not at the things which are seen, but at the things which are not seen; for the things which are seen are temporal, but the things which are not seen are eternal. For we know that if our earthly tent (he's talking about our bodies), our earthly tent which is our house is torn down, we have a building from God, a house not made with hands, eternal in the heavens. For indeed in this house we groan ..."

How many people groaned this morning? You got out of bed. It's a groan. I asked Debbie one day, "Debbie, do all your joints hurt when you get up in the morning?" She said, "No." And she said, "It's because you played sports. I didn't play sports. Nerds age better." That's what she told me.

"For indeed in this house we groan, longing to be clothed with our dwelling from heaven, inasmuch as we, having put it on, shall not be found naked. For indeed while we are in this tent (in this body) we groan, being burdened, because we do not want to be unclothed but to be clothed, in order that what is mortal may be swallowed up by life." He's talking about getting your new body. One day, this mortal will put on immortality, and this perishable will put on the imperishable glorified body. He goes on to say in verse 5, "Now He who prepared us for this very purpose is God, who gave to us the Spirit as a pledge." The word *pledge* is the Greek word arrhabon, and that means "a down payment." Think of it like an engagement ring. God has given us His Spirit as an engagement ring. The engagement ring of His Holy Spirit lets us know that He is coming back to get us, the bride of Christ. He is coming back to take His bride to the Father's house (John 14) and the marriage supper of the Lamb (see Revelation 19).

Then he says in verse 6 and following, "Therefore, being always of good courage, and knowing that while we are at home in the body, we are absent from the Lord – for we walk by faith, not by sight – we are of good courage, I say, and prefer rather to be absent from the body and to be at home with the Lord. Therefore, also we have as our ambition, whether at home or absent, to be pleasing to Him. For we must all appear before the Judgment Seat of Christ, that each one may be recompensed for his deeds in the body, according to what he has done, whether good or bad (worthless)."

I want to share with you three encouragements from this passage—encouragements for those of us who are certain that our final destination is heaven; who are certain that our names are written in the Lamb's Book of Life; who believe the promise in 1 John 2:25, "This is the promise that He Himself has made to us: eternal life." It's a promise from God to all who repent and believe. And He wants us to know that we know that we know that we know that we belong to Him. "He who has the Son has the life; he who does not have the Son of God, does not have the life. These things I have written to you who believe in the name of the Son of God, in order that you may *know* that you have eternal life" (1 John 5:12-13).

Encouragement number one: The assurance of heaven changes our perspective on problems. We look at it from a different lens when we know that our names are written in the Lamb's Book of Life; when we know that heaven is our final destination.

Now, 2 Corinthians 4:16-17 in the Easy-to-Read version says: "That is why we never give up. Our physical body is becoming older and weaker, but our Spirit inside us is made new every day. We have small troubles for a while now, but these troubles are helping us gain an eternal glory. That eternal glory is much greater than our troubles." Paul goes on to say, in chapter 5, verse 1, "For we know, that if the earthly tent, which is our house, is torn down we have a building from God." We know that. That's going back to 1 Corinthians 15. "Remember, gang, I taught you that," Paul says, "and we know this to be true."

Now when it comes to troubles and problems in life, everybody has them. You have problems. I have problems. Paul had problems.. No one is exempt from the troubles and trials of life. It's just part and parcel of the human existence. Jesus said in John 16:33, "In the world you have tribulation, but take courage; I have overcome the world." Job said, "Man is born for trouble, as sparks fly upward" (Job 5:7). That's just the way it is. But when heaven is your final destination, and you have full assurance, it changes how you look at problems.

First of all, we know that God is at work in our problems. Paul had lots of problems. We say everybody's got problems, but I think Paul has us beat on problems. He had tons of them. He was persecuted relentlessly throughout his ministry. In Acts chapter 9, Ananias was reluctant to go see Paul in Damascus because he was Saul of Tarsus, the persecutor of Christians. Ananias said to the Lord, "That guy has done much harm to the saints." But the Lord said to him, "Go, for he is a chosen instrument of Mine, to bear My name before the Gentiles and kings and the sons of Israel; for I will show him how much he must suffer for My name's sake" (Acts 9:15-16). And Paul surely did suffer for the Lord's name. But he saw his difficulties in a different way. He saw his sufferings as "momentary, light affliction." In Paul's mind, they were small problems that were producing an eternal weight of glory. So let's see some of the *small problems* he had.

In 2 Corinthians 11:24 and following, we read, "Five times I received from the Jews thirty-nine lashes. Three times I was beaten with rods, once I was stoned." (Note, he was hit with stones. He's not confessing he had a problem there with marijuana.) "Three times I was shipwrecked, a night and a day I have spent in the deep." (Can you imagine? I've been on the Mediterranean Sea on a couple of occasions. Can you imagine spending a night and a day in the deep blue sea? You know, one thing that

Paul had going for him—he had not seen the movie, *Jaws*. Because a day and a night in the deep, after you've seen *Jaws*, would be horrific.) "I have been on frequent journeys, in dangers from rivers, dangers from robbers, dangers from my countrymen, dangers from the Gentiles, dangers in the city, dangers in the wilderness, dangers on the sea, dangers among false brethren; I have been in labor and hardship, through many sleepless nights, in hunger and thirst, often without food, in cold and exposure." And he calls all of these major issues "momentary, light affliction" —small problems that were producing an eternal weight of glory.

God is at work in the problems. Romans 8:28, "And we know that God causes all things to work together for good ..." Not some things. Not most things. But all things! Good things, bad things, sweet things, sorrowful things and even sinful things, God works all things together for good" "to those who love God, to those who are called according to His purpose." When heaven is on your horizon, you just know, as you're going through difficulties, that God is using this in your life. James 1:2-3, "Consider it all joy when you encounter various trials, knowing that the testing of your faith produces endurance.

And let endurance have its perfect result, that you may be perfect and complete, lacking in nothing." God is at work, and God is going to use the difficulties you have faced, are facing, and will face in the future for good.

Secondly: Because heaven is on the horizon, not only do we know that God is at work; we know that the best is yet to come. Charles Spurgeon, the great preacher in England in the 1800s said, "The best moment of a Christian's life is his last moment because it's the one that is nearest heaven." That's the best moment of your life because in the next moment you're in heaven. What a great perspective! Hey, we know that God is at work in all our difficulties. He's working those together for His glory and our good. And we know that the best is yet to come. Paul says in Romans 8:18, "For I consider that the sufferings of this present life are not worthy to be compared with the glory that is to be revealed to us."

When I do a funeral, I often talk to the crowd about breathing your last on earth and your first in heaven. When I do a funeral for somebody that I know is a believer, I say, "You know, there's a transition that takes place. There's one final breath on earth, and there's a first breath in heaven." I always think of the wonderful song that was written by Don Wyrtzen, *Finally Home.* The lyrics read, *"When surrounded by the blackness of the darkest night, Oh how lonely death can be. At the end of this long tunnel is the shining light, for death is swallowed up in victory. But just think of stepping on shore and finding it Heaven, Of touching a hand and finding it God's, Of breathing new air and finding it Celestial, Of waking up in Glory and finding it Home."* That's what's in store for every Christian! And that truth changes your perspective on problems because you know that God is at work, and momentary light affliction is producing for us an eternal weight of glory far beyond all comparison. The best is yet to come for the child of God.

Encouragement number two: The assurance of heaven takes away the fear of death. Now, it is true that people fear death. I mean, we can try and pretend that people don't, but they do. And the Scripture talks about this in the Book of Hebrews: "Since then the children share in flesh and blood, He Himself likewise also partook of the same ..." He became a human being because we are human beings. He took on flesh and blood, "... that through death He might render powerless him who had the power of death; that is, the devil, and might deliver those who through fear of death were subject to slavery all their lives" (Hebrews 2:14-15). Do you see it? The fear of death is a real issue for human beings. But when you give your heart and life to Christ, He takes the fear out of death. As the song, "In Christ Alone," so masterfully says, *"No guilt in life, no fear in death, this is the power of Christ in me."* I heard Dr. Adrian Rogers say one time, "I've never met a true Christian who's afraid to die. I've met some who are ashamed to die and stand before the Lord, but I've never met a true Christian who is afraid to die—because he knows that the Lord has taken the sting out of death."

So, what happens to a Christian when he dies, when she dies? Well, the Bible makes it clear in 2 Corinthians 5:8 that when we are absent from the body, we are immediately present with the Lord. We go directly to Jesus. There's not a waiting period. There's not a holding area where you're going to be waiting for the Lord's return before you can go to heaven. In Paul's case, he would be in the waiting room since his death in the late 60s AD. That's a long time waiting! But Paul says, "To be absent from the body is to be present with the Lord." He had the desire to depart and be with Christ, for that is very much better. So, when a Christian dies, BOOM, he goes to be with the Lord.

When Jesus saved the repentant thief on the cross, He said, "Truly I say to you, today you shall be with Me in Paradise" (Luke 23:43). It's one of those "truly" statements that we read so often in John's gospel. Truly means "hey, pay attention! This is important! This is fully trustworthy. Hang on to this! "Truly I say to you, today you shall be with Me in Paradise." Now some people teach a soul sleep for the child of God who dies in the Lord. They say, "Well, you know, the Bible talks about falling asleep. Stephen, when he was stoned in Acts 7, 'fell asleep.'" Falling asleep is just a euphemism for dying. Stephen, when he was stoned to death, he said, "I see Jesus standing at the right hand of God." Now, that's significant, because when Jesus ascended to heaven, He sat down at the right hand of God. But Stephen saw Him standing up—a standing ovation if you will—because Stephen had been faithful in preaching Christ, even amidst the stones. And he said as he died, "Lord Jesus, receive my spirit." What happens when a Christian dies? Your soul, your spirit, immediately goes to be with the Lord. Your body goes into the grave. Your body goes into the ground, or it goes into the crematorium, or it goes into the sea. Your soul and spirit are separated from your body. We're brought back together again when we get our glorified bodies at the rapture of the church. First Corinthians chapter 15 and 1 Thessalonians chapter 4 both speak of the rapture, and they speak of God bringing body, soul, and spirit back together in a new, glorified body. When a Christian dies, he doesn't go to soul sleep along with his body. His soul and spirit go to be with the Lord.

And we go to be "at home" with Jesus. See, that's what it says in verse 8, "We are of good courage, I say, and prefer rather to be absent from the body and to be at home with the Lord." That word *home, endemeo* in the Greek, means "to be among one's own people, among one's own country." Think about that for a minute. Are the people of God your own people?

If you conduct a man on the street interview, asking random people, "Do you want to go to heaven when you die?" The answer you will almost always get is, "Yes!". But most everyone else wants to go to heaven when they die—and thinks they will, by hook or by crook. Here is the kicker: will you be at home with the Lord there? Will you be comfortably at home with the Lord and His family?

How can you tell if you are truly on the highway to heaven? One telltale sign is your love for the Lord and His blood-bought children. You're at home with the family of God. You love to come to worship. You love to read the Bible and talk to God in prayer. It doesn't mean you do it all the time. But it does mean that spending time with God and the people of God is a joy and not a chore, a blessing not a burden. It means you are in your element when you are among Christians.

I was 17-years-old when I became a Christian. Before I became a Christian, I never hung out with Christians. Why? It is because I thought those people were weird. They seemed like religious nut jobs. They were just so fanatical about Jesus. I thought to myself, *Lighten up!* Do you know where I was comfortable before I became a Christian? I was comfortable with my unsaved buddies, drinking beer, chasing girls, playing basketball, and living for pleasure. The beer drinking, unsaved jock crowd was where I felt at home. That was my home crowd, not the people of God. But then I got saved. The Lord came to live in my life through the person of the Holy Spirit—and everything changed for me. My wants changed. I wanted to be worshiping God with the people of God. They were and are my brothers and sisters in the Lord. I wanted to be in the presence of God and His family. One way to tell if you have been truly saved is to see if your wants have changed. Listen, if you don't want to worship, you don't want to grow closer to the Lord, and you don't want to be with the people of God, you would not like heaven because heaven is the home of God and His family. David said in Psalm 16:3, "As for the saints who are in the earth, they are the majestic ones in whom is all my delight." He loved the people of God. Remember the words to that old song, "The world is not my home; I'm just passing through. My treasures are laid up somewhere beyond the blue. The angels beckon me from heaven's open door. And I can't feel at home in this world anymore." I am living with heaven on my horizon.

Encouragement number three: The assurance of heaven reminds us of the Bema Judgment. You say, "What is that, the Bema Judgment?" It's spelled B-E-M-A, but it's pronounced in Greek, *Bayma*. It is found in 2 Corinthians 5:10, "For we must all appear (he's talking to Christians), we must all appear before the Judgment Seat of Christ (the Bema of Christ), that each one may be recompensed for his deeds in the body according to what he has done, whether good or bad." Romans 14:10 and 14:12 speak of this judgment also: "For we shall all stand before the Judgment Seat of God, so then each one of us shall give an account of himself to God." We're going to stand before the Bema of God one day. Now, the Bema was a raised platform. They have one in Corinth. When I went to Corinth, I saw the very spot spoken of in Acts 18 where the magistrate took his place on the Bema. That's a special place where the city official would sit to render his judgments. It's the place where speeches would be given. And it was also the place where returning victors in the field of athletics or the field of war would come to receive their awards and rewards for service well done. The Bema Judgment is what every Christian has in his/her future.

Notice that this judgment if only for Christians. God has two judgments for all people. You're going to be in one of two judgments—and there's no getting around it. So, if you give your heart and life to Christ, you're going to stand one day before the Bema Judgment, the Judgment Seat of Christ, and He is going to judge you. If you don't receive Christ as Savior and Lord, then at the end of it all (Revelation 20:11-15), you're going to stand at the Great White Throne Judgment. Remember, everyone at the Great

White Throne Judgment is going into the lake of fire. They're going to be judged according to their deeds. Hell is not the same for every person. Hell is awful for everyone, but there are degrees of hell.

Conversely, for the believer in Jesus, everyone who stands at the Bema is going to heaven. "For no man can lay a foundation other than the one which is laid, which is Jesus Christ" (1 Corinthians 3:11). Every Christian has the foundation of Christ in his/her heart. And every Christian is going to stand before the Lord Jesus to be evaluated—not to determine your destination, but to determine your rewards or lack thereof. The Bema Judgment is a judgment of a Christian's works. The Lord doesn't look at your life from the time you were born until the time you are dead. He looks at your life from the time that you were born-again until the time you died. He looks at what you did as a Christian, what you did with your Christian life.

Now, everyone at the Great White Throne Judgment will experience a judgment of *condemnation*. Everyone who goes to the Bema Judgment will experience a judgment of *commendation*. The Bema is a judgment to determine rewards. And you're going to stand before the

Lord Jesus Christ to give an account to your Savior. "So then, each one will give an account of himself to God" (Romans 14:12).

Do you remember the parable of the talents found in Matthew 25:14-30? The parable goes like this (I paraphrase): A very wealthy man went away on a journey. He entrusted his possessions to his slaves. To one, he gave five talents. (The talent is a sum of money. It's a weight. It's 60 to 80 lbs. So, a talent of silver or a talent of gold, especially gold, would constitute big money.) To another, he gave two talents. To the third, he gave one talent. He said to his slaves, "Do business with this until I return." When he returns, he has a meeting with each slave so that each one can give an account of what he did with what he had been given. That is the Bema Judgment in a nutshell. Every believer in Jesus is going to have a one-on-one meeting with the Lord: "What did you do with what I gave you? What did you do with the time that I gave you? What did you do with the treasure that I gave you? What did you do with the talent that I gave you? What did you do with the spiritual gifts that I gave you? What did you do with the opportunities that I had come your way?"

We are going to have to give an account to the Lord of two main things: (1) what we did with what He gave us, and (2) why we did what we did. We're going to have to give an account of our actions and our motives. The Bible says in 1 Corinthians 4:5, "Therefore, do not go on passing judgment before the time, but wait until the Lord comes who will bring both to light the things hidden in the darkness and disclose the motives of men's hearts, and then each man's praise will come to him from God." At the Judgment Seat of Christ, our Lord, whose eyes are as a flame of fire (Revelation 19:12), He's going to look at us with His all-penetrating, all-knowing gaze. He will thoroughly and perfectly evaluate our service to Him.

The Scripture tells us, "For we must all appear ..." (2 Corinthians 5:10). The word appear, *phaneroo* in Greek, means "to be exposed." We must all be exposed before the Lord at the Bema Judgment and to be recompensed according to what we have done as a Christian, whether good or bad. Now the word for bad, *phaulos*, can also be translated *worthless*. I think that *worthless* best captures the meaning here. Paul said in 1 Corinthians 3:11 and following, "For no man can lay a foundation other than the one which is laid, which is Jesus Christ. Now if any man builds upon the foundation with gold, silver, precious stones (those are good things), wood, hay, straw (those are worthless things), each man's work will become evident, for the day will show it because it is to be revealed with fire, and the fire itself will test the quality of each man's work. If any man's work which he has built upon it remains, he shall receive a reward. If any man's work is burned up, he shall suffer loss, but he himself shall be saved, yet so as through fire."

Have you ever heard somebody say, "Well, all I'm interested in is going to heaven. In John 14, Jesus said, 'In My Father's house are many mansions.' I don't need to have a mansion in heaven to be happy. I can just have a shack by the railroad tracks of heaven. I am fine with that, so long as I am in heaven." There is plenty wrong with this sentiment. First of all, the translation of "mansions" in John 14:2 is a misleading translation. The word *mone* in Greek means *dwelling places.* "In My Father's house are many dwelling places, many apartments. If it were not so, I would have told you." There is only one mansion in heaven. It is called the "Father's house." Furthermore, who wants to go to heaven by the skin of his/her teeth? Who would want to squander all the opportunities the Lord gives us for reward? Why on earth would you be okay with wasting your five talents, two talents, or one talent? Jesus is not okay with that gross dereliction of duty. He is honored when we use what He has given us for His glory. He is insulted, however, when we waste what He has entrusted to us.

In the parable of the talents, the master returns and evaluates each of his slaves. The guy given the five talents said, "Master, you entrusted me with five talents. See, I made five more." And the master says, "Well done, good and faithful slave. You were faithful with a few things. I will put you in charge of many things; enter into the joy of your master" (Matthew 25:21). The slave given the two talents was next to give an account. He said, "Master, you entrusted two talents to me. See, I have gained two more talents." The master responds to him in the exact same way he responded to the first slave, "Well done, good and faithful slave. You were faithful with a few things, I will put you in charge of many things; enter into the joy of your master" (Matthew 25:23).

Let's get real. Don't you want to be one of those two guys? Don't you want to be able to say to the Master,

"Lord, I used what You gave me to Your glory"? Surely, you don't want to be the third slave who buried his talent in the ground. He did nothing with what the master gave him. He wasted it. Perhaps he was bitter that the other two received more than he did. Perhaps he was just lazy. We cannot say for certain, but we do know by his own confession that he thought very poorly of his master. When the time came for him to give an accounting of his activities, he said, "Master, I knew you to be a hard man, reaping where you did not sow, and gathering where you scattered no seed. And I was afraid, and went away and hid your talent in the ground; see, you have what is yours" (Matthew 25:24-25). This is a shockingly insulting response.

First of all, if you gather where you scattered no seed, you're a thief. Anybody who reaps where he doesn't sow is reaping somebody else's property and somebody else's fruit and somebody else's grain. That's called stealing. That's called thievery. This sorry excuse for a slave accuses the master of being a thief. Secondly, he calls his master "a hard man." This means he thinks the master is hard to get along with and hard to please. He sees his master as a crotchety old nitpicker who always finds fault.

A man who can never be satisfied with another's work. He greatly misunderstands the master and greatly insults him.

The master responds to him with these bone-chilling words:

> "You wicked, lazy slave, you knew that I reap where I did not sow, and gather where I scattered no seed. Then you ought to have put my money in the bank, and on my arrival I would have received my money back with interest. Therefore take away the talent from him, and give it to the one who has the ten talents. For to everyone who has shall more be given, and he shall have an abundance; but from the one who does not have, even what he does have shall be taken away. And cast out the worthless slave into the outer darkness; in that place there shall be weeping and gnashing of teeth."
> (Matthew 25:26-30)

This is serious language. Obviously, the master is very angry with his wicked, lazy servant. Since he did not use what was entrusted to him, but lazily buried it in the ground, he lost what was entrusted to him. Did this man lose his salvation? No. This parable teaches us about rewards and loss of rewards. It is not about salvation. The point is simply this: the Lord takes no pleasure in us if we squander the resources He has given to us. We will be big time losers at the Bema Judgment if we have nothing to show for our life as a Christian.

Paul says in 2 Corinthians 5:9, "We have as our ambition, whether absent or present, to be pleasing to the Lord." We want to please the Lord. And so, if you have as your ambition to please the Lord, you want to be able to stand at the Bema Judgment and say, "Master, this is what You gave me, and this is how I used it to glorify your name." And, no doubt, as the Lord looks at every single one of us, we're all going to see things burn up in our lives. You know, it's interesting, wood, hay, and straw aren't worthless in and of themselves. I mean, our houses, for most of us, are built with wood. Wood is a good thing, but it's not good when you test it by fire. Wood gets burned up. Hay is a good thing. You know, you feed cattle with hay and your horses with hay. Hay is a good thing, but it's not good when there's a fire because it's burned up. You make bricks with straw. Just ask Moses and the gang. They wanted to have straw so they could make bricks for Pharaoh. You can make straw hats with straw. You can do stuff with straw, but it's not good when you test it with fire. Only the gold, silver, and precious stones make it through the fire of the Bema Judgment.

Now, if you have as your desire to please the Lord, there's no way in the world you would ever think it's okay to live in a shack on the outskirts of heaven because you would displease the One who died for you in agony and blood. Can you imagine standing before the Lord at the Bema Judgment to have everything in your heart and life exposed? All your hidden motives will be exposed. We can do good things (preaching, teaching, serving, giving, etc.) but with wrong, selfish, greedy motives. In such a case, that good thing becomes wood, hay, and straw. There is no reward when a good thing is done with a bad motive. That's what Jesus got on the religious leaders about. Their motives were rotten to the core. They prayed long prayers just for appearance's sake. They did all this 'spiritual' stuff to be noticed by men. So, that was the extent of their reward— they were noticed by men. But they were going to get no commendation from the Lord.

Even so, we also can do good and godly things but with bad motives. We can serve for the glory of self rather than the glory of God. Psalm 115:1 reminds us, "Not to us, O LORD, not to us, but to Your name give glory because of Your lovingkindness, because of Your truth." And so, God is going to look at our lives and examine our lives. And you say, "This is making me nervous to stand before the Lord." Good! It makes me nervous, too. The very next verse following the text of the Bema Judgment is 2 Corinthians 5:11, "Therefore knowing the fear of the Lord, we persuade men ..." The Bema Judgment should put a little fear in our hearts. "For our God is a consuming fire" (Hebrews 12:29).

Dr. Paige Patterson, the learned theologian who is often maligned, slandered, and falsely accused, is a dear friend of mine. I was conversing with him one day about the Bema Judgment. I said to Dr. P., "I just read Erwin Lutzer's book on *Eternal Rewards: The Tears and Triumphs at the Judgment Seat of Christ.* The more I study the Judgment Seat of Christ, the more nervous and afraid I get about standing before the Lord." He responded, "Me, too." "Therefore knowing the fear of the Lord, we persuade men ..."

I used to think that the Judgment Seat of Christ was akin to an awards dinner. I was in sales for a good number of years before the Lord called me to preach. I worked for Nalco Chemical Company from 1988 - 1997. During my professional sales career at Nalco, we would have the annual sales meeting every February. There would always be an awards dinner. The division managers would recognize and honor the individuals who excelled in the previous year just completed. If you sold at a certain level, you would be highlighted as a top performer. By God's grace, I was blessed with some outstanding sales. Whenever I had an exceptionally good year, I would look forward with anticipation to the upcoming annual meeting. I knew the sales numbers I posted would garner accolades and awards from the national managers. One year, I was awarded an expensive briefcase. It was five hundred dollars in 1990s money. I was happy to get it, but I thought the price was insane. I remember talking to a friend of mine. I said, "Yeah, I won this fancy leather briefcase. It cost five hundred dollars! What idiot would spend five hundred dollars on a briefcase?" He said, "I have one of those." "Oh," I said sheepishly. "You are the idiot. My apologies."

Well, I would read 2 Corinthians 5:10-11 and think those two verses did not go together. Why would anyone who is living for the Lord be fearful of the Judgment Seat of Christ? Here's what Dr. Erwin Lutzer said in his book on this subject, "If we overdo the sorrow aspect of the Bema, we make heaven into hell. But if we underdo it, we make faithfulness inconsequential." There's a tension between those two extremes. We are to have a healthy fear of standing before God one day to give an account of our lives. Remember, "There is no creature hidden from His sight, but all things are open and laid bare to the eyes of Him with whom we have to do" (Hebrews 4:13). When the Lord looks at the depth of your soul and mine with His eyes of flame, it is only right to be in great awe and respect of that day. God forbid that we should ever view it as anything less than a holy, revealing encounter with the King of kings.

Now, the question often arises, "Are we going to see the shame of all our sins committed as Christians at the Bema Judgment?" Of course not. All our sinful deeds were paid in full by the blood of the Lamb. Romans 8:1 tells us, "There is therefore no condemnation for those who are in Christ Jesus." We are not going to have to watch our sins parade before the Lord. But we will have to face the fire of wasted opportunities and combustible motives.

George Whitfield was a great preacher in the 1700s. He said he wanted this on his epitaph: "Here lies George Whitfield; what sort of man he was, the great day will discover." When God reveals the things hidden in the darkness and discloses motives of men's hearts, then each man's praise will come to him from God.

In 1992, Billy Graham was being interviewed by Diane Sawyer on the subject of death. Billy said when he died, he wanted to hear the Lord say, "Well done, my good and faithful slave." But he followed that up by adding, "That's what I want to hear, but I'm not sure I'm going to hear it." When I saw that for the very first time, I said, "Good night! If Billy Graham doesn't hear, "Well done, good and faithful slave," what hope do I have?" But here's the thing to glean from that interview: Billy Graham, although used by God to lead millions to faith in Christ, didn't presume upon anything. He knew the darkness in his own heart. He knew the sins that he struggled with, the selfish motives he wrestled with. And he knew when everything came to the light of the Lord, then the true quality of his life and ministry would be revealed.

Do you long to hear the Lord say to you at the Bema Judgment, "Well done, good and faithful slave." (It's not to be translated servant. The Greek word is *doulos*, a slave.) Paul said, "We have as our ambition, whether at home or absent, to be pleasing to Him." A little poem by C. T. Studd brings this point home: "Only one life, twill soon be past; only what's done for Christ will last." Amy Carmichael said, "We have all eternity to celebrate the victories, but only a few hours before sunset to win them."

Lastly, remember that at the Judgment Seat of Christ everything is set for all eternity, the rewards are fixed. When God puts the flame to your life, whatever is left—if there's gold, if there's silver, if there's precious stone—is the reward of your life on earth as a believer. And God is a very generous rewarder. But if there's nothing left, you yourself shall be saved, "yet so as through fire" (1 Corinthians 3:15). For all eternity, you will have nothing to show for your time as a Christian. You will have no crowns, no rewards to lay at your Master's feet. No wonder the Bible tells us that He wipes every tear from our eyes. I believe there will be more than a few tears at the Judgment Seat of Christ.

John said in 3 John 1:4, "I have no greater joy than this, to hear of my children walking in the truth." Let me tell you, the Lord Jesus has no greater joy than for you and for me to walk with Him, and to stay connected to Him, and to abide in Him, so that He can flow His life through us, so that He can use us to shine for Christ and to share what great things the Lord has done for us, and how He had mercy on us. That is our calling from God. And if we will live this way, we can stand at the Bema Judgment with a healthy, godly fear. We can face the test of fire from the Lord Jesus and see good works done in the power of the Holy Spirit pass the test. We can hear our Savior say, "Well done, my child. You were faithful with a few things; I will put you in charge of many things; enter into the joy of your Master." May we live and serve the King each day, looking forward to the joy of a *well done*!

CHAPTER FOUR

Inheriting Heaven

*... but just as it is written, "THINGS WHICH EYE HAS
NOT SEEN AND EAR HAS NOT HEARD, AND which
HAVE NOT ENTERED THE HEART OF MAN, ALL THAT
GOD HAS PREPARED FOR THOSE WHO LOVE HIM."*
1 Corinthians 2:9

Do you remember the Hollywood classic, *The Wizard of Oz*? It was one of my family's favorite movies when we were growing up. If you are not familiar with the story line, here goes. Dorothy Gale, the main character, is caught in a tornado that lifts her farmhouse in Kansas off the ground and transports her to a strange land "somewhere over the rainbow." It was a very odd and often scary place with munchkins, witches, a yellow-brick road, talking animals and trees, flying monkeys, and a wizard.

Throughout her time in Oz, all Dorothy wants to do is go home. That is her driving motivation. She makes the long and arduous journey to the Emerald City in hopes that the Wizard of Oz could help her get home. He agrees to take her back to Kansas in a hot air balloon. As they are about to take off, Toto, her beloved little dog, sees a cat and jumps from her arms. When she gets out of the basket of the hot air balloon to retrieve him, the craft lifts from the ground, leaving her behind. She is forlorn, thinking she has lost her chance forever to get back home.

When all hope of home seemed lost, the good witch Glinda appears with good news. Dorothy has magic slippers that can take her home. All she had to do was click her heels together three times and say to herself, "There's no place like home. There's no place like home. There's no place like home." Lo and behold, she wakes up in her familiar farmhouse bed in Kansas. She was home!

While it is true that there is no place like home, it is even more true and significant that there is no place like heaven. Heaven is a believer's eternal home!

Christians have long wondered, *what is heaven going to be like*? What do we do in heaven? Our minds just race with questions about heaven. While God certainly tells us in the Bible about this place called heaven, He doesn't give us all the specifics about heaven. But He tells us enough to get us super excited about going there!

Now remember, the Book of Revelation (note that Revelation is singular, not plural) is not the revelation of John; it's the revelation of Jesus Christ that was given to John, the unveiling of Jesus Christ to John. And this revelation is given in stages. In Revelation 1:19, the resurrected Christ tells John, "Write therefore the things which you have seen, and the things which are, and the things which shall take place after these things." In obedience to this command, John writes what he has seen

(Revelation 1), what is currently happening (Revelation 2-3, the seven letters to the seven churches), and what is to come (Revelation 4-22). So, Revelation is divided into these three sections.

I personally believe that the Lord gives us a faint picture of the pretribulation rapture of the church in Revelation 4:1: "After these things I looked, and behold, a door standing open in heaven, and the first voice which I had heard, like the sound of a trumpet speaking with me, said, 'Come up here, and I will show you what must take place after these things.'" John immediately goes from the Island of Patmos directly to heaven as he was caught up in the Spirit to the very throne room of God. Revelation chapters 4 and 5 give us a vivid glimpse of the worship of God that takes place in heaven. It is awe-inspiring!

Revelation chapter 6 brings us the beginning of the Tribulation period. This chilling seven-year period is called "the time of Jacob's trouble" (Jeremiah 30:7). It is the time where the dam of God's mercy gives way to the waters of His great wrath. The Tribulation period is replete with perfect and complete judgment upon a Christ rejecting world. There are seven seals of judgment, seven trumpets of judgment, and seven bowls of judgment. These judgments increase in severity and devastation. In addition, the Antichrist—literally Satan in the flesh—declares himself to be God. He forces the world to worship him and receive the mark of the beast. Those who refuse will be hunted like dogs and slaughtered. The devastation of the Tribulation is beyond comprehension as billions of people die. In fact, Jesus said, "Unless those days had been cut short, no life would have been saved" (Matthew 24:22).

It is very interesting to note that the church is never mentioned during this unprecedented time of hell on earth, recorded in Revelation chapters 6-18. Why do we not read of some encouragement and instructions to the church as they face the Tribulation? The plausible explanation is that the church is not there. The church has been raptured, just as the Bible teaches in John 14:1-3 and 1 Thessalonians 1:10, 4:13-18. No doubt, people—especially Jewish people —are getting saved during the Tribulation. But the church, the bride of Christ, has been snatched away to the Father's house to experience the Bema judgment and the marriage supper of the Lamb. Those in Christ will experience the glories of heaven. Those left behind will experience the horrors of the Tribulation. This is all the more reason to "make your calling and election sure" (2 Peter 1:10).

Now in Revelation chapter 19, we read about the glorious, awesome, and visible return of Christ. He comes back with His bride at the Battle of Armageddon and defeats the Antichrist and his forces with the sharp sword of the Word of God. He literally speaks them into oblivion. The carnage is so great at this epic battle that there is a river of blood up to the horses' bridles for a distance of two hundred miles (Revelation 14:20).

On the heels of this great victory, the Antichrist and false prophet (a demonic counterpart to the Holy Spirit) are thrown into the lake of fire (hell), and Satan is bound for a thousand years so he can no longer deceive the nations (see Revelation 20:1-3). Jesus then sets up His Millennial Kingdom and rules from Jerusalem for a thousand years. Heaven truly comes to earth during the righteous reign of the King of kings.

Note that the Kingdom is inhabited by glorified saints who rule and reign with Christ and unglorified human beings who got saved during the Tribulation and survived the heavenly plagues and the satanic persecution.

The Kingdom has no unbelievers in it at the outset. However, the unglorified saints will be fruitful and multiply and fill the earth with offspring. Every child born in the Kingdom will need to be born again, just like it is today. Even though Jesus is physically present on the earth, ruling from Jerusalem, and even though there is peace and prosperity on earth, and even though the desert blooms like a rose and the curse on earth is removed (it will be like it was in the Garden of Eden before man sinned), many of the children born into the Kingdom will not follow the Lord. At the end of a thousand years, Satan is released from his prison. He instantly deceives those who are not true believers in Christ and leads one last revolt against the Lord and His saints. Satan is defeated yet again and thrown into hell forevermore (see Revelation 20:7-10).

At the end of the Millennial Kingdom and Satan's eternal demise, time ends. Unbelievers are raised for their day in court, known as the Great White Throne Judgment, where they stand trial before the Judge of all the earth. They are found guilty and are sentenced to the lake of fire (Revelation 20:11-15).

The last two chapters of Revelation focus on eternity and our eternal home in heaven. John writes, "And I saw a new heaven and a new earth, for the first heaven and the first earth passed away, and there is no longer any sea. And I saw the holy city, new Jerusalem, coming down out of heaven from God, made ready as a bride adorned for her husband. And I heard a loud voice from the throne, saying, 'Behold, the tabernacle of God is among men, and He shall dwell among them, and they shall be His people, and God Himself shall be among them.' And He shall wipe away every tear from their eyes, and there shall no longer be any death, there shall no longer be any mourning or crying or pain; the first things have passed away. And He who sits on the throne said, 'Behold, I am making all things new.' And He said, 'Write, for these words are faithful and true.' And He said to me, 'It is done. I am the Alpha and the Omega, the beginning and the end. I will give to the one who thirsts from the spring of the water of life without cost. He who overcomes shall inherit these things, and I will be his God and he will be My son'" (Revelation 21:1-7).

So, what is in store for the child of God? As Christians, the Scripture says we're going to "inherit these things." What is our inheritance in the Lord? What is our eternal home in heaven going to be like? Let's look at three wonderful characteristics of heaven.

Number one: Heaven is beyond our imagination. Paul said in 1 Corinthians 2:9, "THINGS WHICH EYE HAS NOT SEEN AND EAR HAS NOT HEARD, AND WHICH HAVE NOT ENTERED THE HEART OF MAN, ALL THAT GOD HAS PREPARED FOR THOSE WHO LOVE HIM."

Now, John is going to try to describe heaven, but it's a tall task. He is describing something that is indescribable. Heaven is far greater than our minds can comprehend. When Paul was caught up to heaven, he stated, "I know a man in Christ who fourteen years ago—whether in the body, I do not know, or out of the body I do not know, God knows—such a man was caught up to heaven" (2 Corinthians 12:2). Obviously, Paul is talking about himself. He was caught to the third heaven. He went through the atmospheric heaven and the planetary heaven to the third heaven, the place where God lives. He goes on to say, "And I know how such a man—whether in the body or apart from the body I do not know, God knows—was caught up into Paradise, and heard inexpressible words, which a man is not permitted to speak" (2 Corinthians 12:3-4). Paul never talked about what he saw and what he heard. He said, "I heard words that are inexpressible. I can't talk about them." Well, John talks about them. But he has trouble describing that which is indescribable, as you can understand. John says, "I saw a new heaven and a new earth; for the first heaven and the first earth passed away, and there is no longer any sea."

So, the first thing we learn about our eternal home in heaven is the newness of it. It is brand new. Many people are so concerned today about the hoax known as Climate Change. One very ill-informed politician even claimed in 2019 that the earth will be no more in twelve years (2031) unless we make austere (and disastrous) course corrections on our carbon dioxide emissions. Are we really in danger of destroying the planet? Nonsense! God controls the climate and the future of planet earth. Surely, we are not to unduly pollute the planet and destroy rivers, lakes, streams, and oceans with toxic waste. We are to behave responsibly and not stupidly as it relates to the planet. But the simple fact is this: planet earth is going to be around for as long as God wants it to be around. Once it has fulfilled its purpose, God will let it pass away and make a new one for us. "I saw a new heaven and a new earth, for the first heaven and the first earth passed away." They died, so to speak. They're gone. And God makes it brand new. The word for new, *kainos*, means "new in quality." The Lord says in Revelation 21:5, "Behold, I am making all things new (kainos)." It's going to be new in quality. It's not going to be anything that you and I currently know because it's brand new. John communicates this truth by saying, "… and there's no longer any sea."

Remember, John is on the island of Patmos. He's exiled on the Alcatraz Island of his day. The island of Patmos is relatively small—about thirteen square miles in total. All that John sees from this island is water from the Aegean Sea. He is separated from his loved ones by water. The oceans cover over 70% of the surface of the earth. But in this new heaven and new earth you don't have any waters that separate. It's not a water-based world. And so, it is different than what it was before. God makes it new, brand new. He doesn't just do an extreme makeover akin to Chip and Joanna Gaines on the show *Fixer Upper*. No, God makes the new heaven and earth brand new and different from anything we have ever seen or experienced.

The new heaven and the new earth serve as God's greatest creative masterpiece (outside of humanity). The crown jewel of the new heaven and the new earth is the holy city, new Jerusalem. Verse 2 states, "And I saw the holy city new Jerusalem, coming down out of heaven from God, made ready as a bride adorned for her husband." That's the capital city that comes down out of that third heaven to this new earth and heaven that God makes. The capital city is the new Jerusalem, and it is exquisite. I mean, it is one amazing, jaw-dropping place. The Scripture says that it's "made ready as a bride adorned for her husband." In John 14, where Jesus said, "Let not your heart be troubled. Believe in God, believe also in Me. In My Father's house are many dwelling places. If it were not so, I would have told you, for I go to prepare a place for you ..." The place He was talking about is the new Jerusalem, the capital city of heaven. The new Jerusalem is the place with streets of gold, gates of pearl, and dimensions of a cube— fifteen hundred miles in length, width, and in height.

It is prepared as a bride adorns herself for her husband. As a father of three daughters who have all been married, I know about brides getting ready for their wedding day. To be sure, it is a big deal for a bride. The bride arrives at the church (along with her attendants) five or six hours before the service to give themselves time to get ready with hair, make-up, clothing, and accessories. It takes a bride a long time to prepare herself. Do you know why? It is because she is going to pull out all the stops to look as beautiful as humanly possible on her wedding day. She is a bride adorned for her husband. She wants to do all she can to look her absolute best for him.

What does God do with the new Jerusalem? He pulls out all the stops. He spares no expense. He cuts no corners. He prepares a place for His people that will blow our minds and take our breath away.

Furthermore, the new Jerusalem is very large—a fifteen-hundred-mile cube. That equates to a surface area roughly half the size of the United States. But it is also fifteen hundred miles high. If you were to think of the new Jerusalem as a high rise building, It would be five hundred floors, with each floor as broad as half of America with a three mile high ceiling. Mark it down, the Father's house is "a big, big house with lots and lots of rooms." It is some kind of place. A city more beautiful and abundant than we can possibly comprehend.

Verse two calls it "the holy city." There has always been something special and sacred about Jerusalem. It's "the city of the great King" (Psalm 48:2). God loves Jerusalem. And God put Jerusalem in David's heart early in his life. Now Jerusalem, the city of peace, was formerly called Jebus. It was home to the Jebusites. In the Book of Joshua, Jebus was one of the cities in the Promised Land that the Jews never conquered. It appeared to be an impregnable city—"the stronghold of Zion" (2 Samuel 5:7). But when David defeated Goliath in 1 Samuel 17, he took Goliath's severed head to Jebus/Jerusalem. I think that was his way of saying, "Do you Jebusites see this? Well, you're next!" And when David was installed as King of all the twelve tribes of Israel a good number of years later, he overthrew the Jebusites and conquered the seemingly unconquerable city. From that point on, Jerusalem was the capital city of God's people.

In Revelation 21:2, we read of the "new Jerusalem." Old Jerusalem was tainted by sin. The Lord abandoned His temple in Jerusalem. Jesus said to the Jewish religious leaders a few months before His crucifixion, "Behold, your house is left to you desolate" (Luke 13:35). In 70 AD, old Jerusalem and the beautiful temple were utterly decimated by the Romans. In the coming Tribulation Period, the temple will be rebuilt in old Jerusalem. This time the pollution of the temple and the city will be unmatched as the Antichrist "takes his seat in the temple of God, displaying himself as being God" (2 Thessalonians 2:4). Jesus called this coming occurrence, "the abomination of desolation" (Matthew 24:15). Suffice it to say, old Jerusalem may be the beloved city, but it is stained with sin and degradation.

So, God has a new Jerusalem for all eternity. This city is holy, untainted by sin. We could almost say that it is holy, holy, holy. It's holy because God is there. It's holy because it's dedicated to His glory. And it's holy because the only people who will ever enter and occupy the new Jerusalem are those who love Jesus, trust Jesus, and have been washed white as snow in the blood of Jesus. Revelation 21:27 reminds us, "And nothing unclean, and no one who practices abomination and lying, shall ever come into it, but only those whose names are written in the Lamb's book of life."

John saw the new heaven and the new earth. He saw the holy city, the new Jerusalem. He saw that which is more beautiful and awesome than our minds can comprehend.

Second characteristic: Heaven is nothing like now. It is hard to have a reference point for heaven because it will be nothing like life on earth is now. Revelation 21:4 reads, "And He shall wipe away every tear from their eyes, and there shall no longer be any death, there shall no longer be any mourning or crying or pain; the first things have passed away."

So, how does John describe heaven, the indescribable? He describes it by saying what's not there. He mentions the blessed exemptions—the things that are no longer present. Death and mourning and crying and pain are all part of the human experience on earth, but they don't exist in heaven.

In the eternal state of heaven, there will never be one second of sorrow, not one second. There will not be anything in heaven that would cause us to shed tears.

I believe, however, that at the Judgment Seat of Christ there may be tears of regret for those who wasted their Christian lives on trivial pursuits. And I believe that the Lord does wipe away those tears at the Bema Judgment. But Revelation 21 and 22 deal with the eternal state. The Judgment Seat of Christ takes place before the eternal state. All that happened before is now passed. We have entered into eternity where there is no sorrow, no suffering, no death, and no tears. All those former things are gone.

People often ask the question, "Will we remember friends and loved ones that didn't go to heaven?" I mean, how can heaven be constant bliss for us if we remember a son, a daughter, a parent, a loved one, or a friend who is in hell? Are we going to remember their plight for all eternity? Surely, that would bring sorrow to our heart. But since there is no sorrow in heaven, how can this be reconciled? Remember, we will have the mind of Christ in heaven. We will see things the way He does, and we will feel about things as He does. The Lord is not sorrowful in heaven. He is not eternally grieving the lost, and neither will we.

Furthermore, there will always be complete joy and satisfaction in heaven. We have new bodies that we're given in heaven—glorified bodies—bodies like the Lord Jesus Christ had when He rose from the dead. "For our citizenship," Paul says, "is in heaven from which we eagerly wait for a Savior, the Lord Jesus Christ, who will transform the body of our humble state into conformity with the body of His glory through the exertion of the power that He has even to subject all things to Himself" (Philippians 3:20-21). We're going to have a body just like Jesus' body, glorious and indestructible. Paul said, "For this perishable must put on the imperishable, and this mortal must put on immortality. But when this perishable will have put on the imperishable, and this mortal will have put on immortality, then will come about the saying that is written, 'DEATH IS SWALLOWED UP in victory. O DEATH WHERE IS YOUR VICTORY? O DEATH WHERE IS YOUR STING?" (1 Corinthians 15:53-55). There is no death in the eternal state. And we have bodies that cannot die, and we will be able to experience joy like we've never experienced before. We'll be able to experience satisfaction like never before. And that's what heaven is. It is complete joy and satisfaction.

Look at verse 6 of chapter 21, "Then He said to me, 'It is done. I am the Alpha and the Omega, the beginning and the end.'" Alpha is the first letter of the Greek alphabet; Omega is the last. "I will give to the one who thirsts from the spring of the water of life without cost." That is God's way of saying, "You will be satisfied in heaven!" In Psalm 16:11, David says, "In Your presence, Lord, is fullness of joy; and in Your right hand there are pleasures forever."

Some people ask, "Well, what are we going to do in heaven? Am I going to get bored in heaven? You're talking about forever and ever and ever and ever." They have this erroneous idea that somehow we become angels. Have you ever heard that?   Somebody says, "Well, you know, Gramma died. Now she's an angel." No, she's not! The Bible does not tell us that when we die, we become angels. If we know Christ as Savior and Lord, then we are sons and daughters of the Most High God. Angels, on the other hand, are heavenly servants. But we are part of the family of God! We don't become angels—and that's a good thing. I would much rather be a beloved son who is a joint heir with Jesus than a beloved servant.

But we have this idea that we get wings and will sit on a cloud playing a harp for all eternity. Well, I would certainly love to be able to play the harp, but that is not the biblical picture of eternal heaven. Playing the harp for all eternity would get monotonous and dull after a few years. And heaven has not one skinny minute of dullness and boredom. It is the most exciting, exhilarating, joyful place God ever created. "In His presence is fullness of joy, and in His right hand there are pleasures forever." You will be satisfied beyond anything you've ever experienced before in your life. And it's not a satisfaction that wanes over time.

The things we can experience on earth are passing pleasures and temporary thrills. Think about going on a great ride at Six Flags or Disney World. The ride is a shot of adrenaline and fun for a few brief minutes. When it is over, the thrill is gone. Heaven is not a brief thrill ride. It is an exhilarating experience that lasts forever and ever. Love, joy, peace, and satisfaction will be full and overflowing in our lives every single day in heaven. How do I know? It is because we will be with God, the source of all joy, peace, and satisfaction.

Now, the opposite experience is hell. The Lord talks about hell in Revelation 21:8, "But for the cowardly and unbelieving and abominable and murderers and immoral persons and sorcerers and idolaters and all liars, their part will be in the lake that burns with fire and brimstone, which is the second death." What do people experience in hell? They will experience torment, loneliness, and frustration to the full. They will be alienated from God and others for all eternity. Hell is filled with weeping, wailing, and gnashing of teeth. It is filled with anger, hatred, guilt, and regret. The differences between heaven and hell could not be more striking.

Characteristic number three: Heaven is living with God forever. That's really what heaven is in a nutshell. His presence is what makes heaven so wonderful. John states, "And I heard a loud voice from the throne, saying, 'Behold, the tabernacle of God is among men, and He will dwell among them, and they shall be His people, and God Himself will be among them" (Revelation 21:3). Make no mistake, it is the Lord that makes heaven eternal bliss.

The Christian musical group of the 1980s, Silverwind, had a song on the radio that I loved. It was titled, *Heaven is Being with You.* The lyrics captured the reason why heaven is heaven:

> *I've heard stories of heaven,*
> *Pavement made of gold,*

Ageless beauty forever,
That never grows old.
But if I got there, only to find out,
Jesus, you were not up there,
Goodbye wings, angel things.

Heaven is being with You,
There's nothing I'd rather do.
There is nothing better,
Knowing you is Heaven,
There is nothing better,
Loving you forever,
Jesus.

Heaven holds all my wishes,
Making dreams come true.
Heaven has to be Jesus,
Just being with You.

There is no laughter,
Or joy in the music.
Jesus, if you are not there,
Then the song is all wrong.

Heaven is being with You,
There's nothing I'd rather do.

There is nothing better,

Knowing you is Heaven,

There is nothing better,

Loving you forever,

Jesus.

We will dwell with God in heaven. The Lord chooses to live with us forever. This was His end game from the time He created Adam and Eve. He wants a redeemed family to live with Him and enjoy Him forever.

Now, there has been a question that theologians kick around. God is spirit. And so, in heaven, do we see God the Father, or do we just see God the Son? See, it says in John 1:18, "No man has seen God at any time; the only begotten God (or "only begotten Son" as some translations say) who is in the bosom of the Father, He has explained Him." Adrian Rogers is one of my all-time favorite preachers. When he preached through Revelation, he asked the question in his sermon, "Will we see God the Father in heaven?" He said, "Friend, the only God you'll see in heaven is the Lord Jesus Christ." As I thought about that statement, I wondered if it was biblically correct. I asked another trusted theologian about it. He said, "Hmm. I really like Adrian, but I don't know if that statement is true. In Revelation 4 and 5, we see someone that sits on the throne, and then the Lamb approaches. Furthermore, in Revelation 21 and 22, the Scripture speaks of the throne of God and of the Lamb. So, what is the answer to the question? Will we see the Father, or will we just see the Father in the Son?

I think that in heaven we get to see God the Father. I think John is talking about God the Father. Of course, God the Son dwells with us; but I think God the Father dwells with us in His fullness also. This is what Paul said to Timothy in 1 Timothy 6:14-16, "… that you keep the commandment without stain or reproach until the appearing of our Lord Jesus Christ, which He will bring about at the proper time—He who is the blessed and only Sovereign, the King of kings and Lord of lords, who alone possess immortality and dwells in unapproachable light, whom no man has seen or can see. To Him be honor and eternal dominion! Amen." God the Father dwells in unapproachable light. He says in Revelation 21:3, "I'm going to dwell among them." Wow! The God who dwells in unapproachable light, the God who no man has seen or can see in his humanity, is going to make Himself visible to us. We're going to dwell with Him.

The Scripture also says that we're going to serve Him. Revelation 22:3, "There shall no longer be any curse; and the throne of God and of the Lamb shall be in it, and His bond-servants shall serve Him." We say, "What do we do in heaven? Is it just one long worship service that lasts forever?" Well, the worship is forever, but it is not like an eternal church service. It's not sitting in a pew for all eternity. Certainly, there will be times of this in heaven, but God loves variety. We will serve the Lord. He will have things for us to do that will be meaningful, satisfying, and fulfilling.

In heaven, we see His face and His full glory. Revelation 22:4-5, "And they shall see His face, and His name shall be on their foreheads. And there shall no longer be any night, and they shall have not need of the light of a lamp nor the light of the sun, because the Lord God shall illumine them, and they shall reign forever and ever." We see His face. See, the apostles saw the face of Jesus. Peter, James, and John saw Jesus in all His power when He went up to the Mount of Transfiguration and unzipped the veil of His flesh. They saw His clothes become white like lightening and His face shining like the sun. They got a glimpse of His glory! In heaven, there is no small glimpse!

We will see the Lord in the fullness of His glory! We will see the Father's face. Wow! We will see the God who dwells in unapproachable light.

In Exodus 33:18, Moses prayed to the LORD, "Show me Your glory." He desired to see God in all His glory and beauty and splendor. God basically replied, "Moses, you can't see My full glory. I'll show you the backside of My glory. I'll show you the edges of My glory. You can't see My face. No man can see My face and live." So, God put Moses in the cleft of the rock. He covered him there with His hand as He passed by and proclaimed the glory of His being, "The LORD, the LORD, God, compassionate and gracious, slow to anger and abounding in lovingkindness and truth; who keeps lovingkindness for thousands, who forgives iniquity, transgression, and sin; yet He will by no means leave the guilty unpunished, visiting the iniquity of fathers on the children and the grandchildren to the third and fourth generations" (Exodus 34:6-7). And Moses made haste to bow low and worship.

Moses was permitted to see just the backside of God's glory. In heaven, we see the full glory of God. We shall see His face! And it's not for a fleeting moment because we will dwell with Him forever and ever!

And you know what's so cool? You read about the new Jerusalem, this fifteen-hundred-mile cube. It's filled with gold and with precious stones, and it does not have need of a light of a lamp, or the light of the sun, because the Lord God lights it up with His glory. And it's just this brilliant, blazing light that comes out of the new Jerusalem, the capital city of heaven. That's where we're going to live. That's the Father's house. Now the new earth is like our backyard, our estate, where we run and play and conduct business for the Master. And when it's time to come in at the end of the day, we enter the house, the new Jerusalem. That is where we live for all eternity. It is going to be so awesome.

Listen! God says in verse 7, "He who overcomes shall inherit these things, and I will be his God and he will be My son." However in verse 8 He warns, "But for the cowardly and unbelieving and abominable and murderers and immoral persons and sorcerers and idolaters and all liars, their part will be in the lake that burns with fire and brimstone, which is the second death." Such a contrast! The person who overcomes, he inherits these things with God. You say, "Well, I don't feel much like an overcomer." Maybe I am not included since it is only for overcomers. Remember 1 John 5:4-5, "For whatever is born of God overcomes the world; and this is the victory that has overcome the world—our faith. And who is the one who overcomes the world, but he who believes that Jesus is the Son of God." What's an overcomer? It is someone who puts his/her faith and trust in Jesus. It's not that you have to be this big, strong person who defies all the odds and overcomes in the power of discipline and determination. No! It's that you put your faith and trust in Jesus. You realize you can't overcome, so you look to Him to be your Savior and Redeemer. It is Jesus who makes you an overcomer by His indwelling Holy Spirit.

You have a choice. You can come to Christ and put your faith and trust in Jesus alone for your salvation. You can confess to God that you're a helpless, hopeless sinner. You can tell Him that you can't save yourself, and you deserve hell for your sins and your rebellion against Him. You can come and say to the Lord, "Jesus, Son of David, have mercy on me. Cleanse me. Save me. Change me. I give myself to You." And the moment that you pray that kind of prayer—and mean it—He saves you.   Romans 10:13 teaches, "WHOEVER WILL CALL UPON THE NAME OF THE LORD WILL BE SAVED." But if you don't come to Him, if you don't call upon His name, if you choose your sin over God's Son, then Revelation 21:8 becomes your eternal future. Your part will be in the lake that burns with fire and brimstone. Revelation 21:27 reminds us that the only people going to heaven are those whose names are written in the Lamb's book of life. Is your name written in His book?

Revelation 22:17 records God's invitation to all people to come to Him while there is time: "And the Spirit and the bride say, 'Come.' And let the one who hears say, 'Come.' And let the one who is thirsty come; let the one who wishes take the water of life without cost." God's favorite word is come. "Come now, and let us reason together, says the LORD. Though your sins be as scarlet, they shall be white as snow. Though they be red like crimson, they shall be as wool" (Isaiah 1:18). Jesus said, "Come to Me, you who are weary and heavy-laden, and I will give you rest" (Matthew 11:28). He will give salvation to those who come to Him in brokenness, humility, repentance, and faith.   Why would anyone fail to come?

Why would anyone blow off the Lord's gracious invitation? It makes no sense to reject Christ. "Come now, and let us reason together, says the LORD ..." It's a reasonable thing to come to Jesus. He's offering you forgiveness and salvation and joy and peace and power and a home forever in heaven with Him. Why would you say no to all of that?

Let me close with this story. Many years ago in the Midwest, there was an old German farmer by the name of Mr. Klein. He was known as Old Man Klein. He never went to church. He was a crusty old guy who lived for sin and self. But one Sunday, he found himself walking down the street in town. He was feeling lonely and depressed about his life. There was no joy, no peace, no future—there was just nothing. He happened to walk past a church where the congregation was singing a hymn. He could faintly hear the words of this hymn, and the lyrics shocked him. The song says, *"Grace! 'tis a charming sound, harmonious to the ear; Heaven with the echo shall resound, and all the earth shall hear. Saved by grace alone, this is all my plea. Jesus died for all mankind, and Jesus died for me."* That's what the song said. But that is not what he heard, He heard these words, *"Jesus died for old man Klein, and Jesus died for me."* All of the sudden, he stopped. "They're singing about me. They said Jesus died for old man Klein. That's me!" And it hit him. "Jesus didn't just die for the world. He died for me." Mr. Klein entered that church, heard the full gospel, and trusted Christ as Savior and Lord. His testimony was simple and profound: "Jesus did die for old man Klein, and Jesus died for me."

Listen! Jesus died for you. If any man's name was not found written in the Book of Life, he was thrown into the lake of fire. God has a place in His Book for you, and He says, "Come. The Spirit and the bride say, 'Come.' And let the one who hears say, 'Come.' And let the one who is thirsty come. And let the one who wishes take the water of life without cost." He paid it all for you. Would you come and give Him your heart and give Him your life? If you do, you will receive the gift of eternal life and spend eternity with God in heaven!